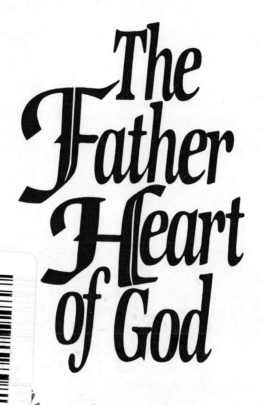

The Father Heart of God

**God Loves You—
Learn to Know His
Compassionate Touch**

FLOYD McCLUNG, JR.

Study Guide development by Sharon Mutchler.

THE FATHER HEART OF GOD

Copyright © 1985 by Floyd McClung, Jr.
Published by Harvest House Publishers
Eugene, Oregon 97402

Library of Congress Catalog Card Number 85-061075
ISBN 0-89081-491-0

Printed in the United States of America.

GRATEFUL ACKNOWLEDGMENTS

I am very grateful for the help and advice of many friends who made it possible for me to write this book.

I am particularly thankful to my wife Sally for her love and encouragement, and to my children, Misha and Matthew, who were very patient with me while I spent many hours working in my study, and to my secretary, Lura Garrido, for typing and retyping the manuscript.

My special thanks also to Linda Patton and Terry Tootle, who helped Lura with the typing, and to Tom Hallas, Roger Forster, and Alv Magnus for the suggestions they made. Thanks to Christine Alexander and Ed Sherman for their research assistance. And I am very grateful to Dr. H. Wayne Light, who is not only a highly trained psychologist but also my cousin and friend, for his suggestions and help in drawing up the guidelines contained in the Appendix.

Many friends encouraged me along the way when I doubted the value of the book or my ability to finish it. I am especially grateful to Henk Rothuizen, Jon Petersen, Arne Wilkening, Wilbert van Laake, John Goodfellow, Lynn Green, Dr. Phil Blakley, and John Kennedy for their timely encouragement and counsel.

I also sincerely appreciate the encouragement I received from Richard Herkes and the people at Kingsway. They have reflected a kingdom attitude in all our dealings together.

I am also indebted to Mike Saia and John Dawson, and to Last Days Ministries for giving permission to use portions of the tract *The Father Heart of God*. This tract is available from Last Days Ministries and can be ordered by writing to them at P.O. Box 40, Lindale, TX 75771, U.S.A.

Most of all I am grateful to the Lord, for all that is good is from Him!

A FRESH LOOK
AT GOD

As my two children, Misha and Matthew, and I studied the painting, we experienced a feeling of great sadness. It covered a very large canvas and was painted in sweeping, childlike strokes. The tall, sticklike figure topped with a huge, square-shaped head was portrayed in dark colors that conveyed a sense of coldness and harshness. The beaklike nose and great protruding arms almost made us feel as if it were a monster.

It was titled "Man," but according to one of the guides at Amsterdam's Stedelijk Museum, the original name of Karel Appel's work was "My Father."

The three of us discussed the painting for a long time. What kind of relationship did Karel Appel have with his father? Even more important, how did that affect his view of God? We wondered if he believed in God, and if so, did he perceive Him as a loving Father?

I have written this book because most people do not know God as a loving Father. They do not think of Him as someone to love and trust, someone who is worthy of their absolute loyalty and commitment. Whether a person is a Christian or not, at one time or another everyone gives serious thought to the question of who God is and what He is like.

Many people long to know God personally but imagine Him to be a remote, impersonal Being who cannot be known. Others yearn for a relationship with Him but cling to the misconception that He sits in heaven wearing a black suit and twisting His long gray beard as He glares down seeking to judge anyone who dares to smile on Sunday.

This book is written to give us a fresh way to look at God, and to help us deal with areas in our lives which can hinder our relationship with Him as our Father. We will explore how past hurts can color our concept of God and how our earthly fathers may have unknowingly influenced our view of our heavenly Father.

We will also consider how we should respond to God if He is indeed a loving Father. It is one thing to talk about God—who He is and what He is like. It is quite another to talk about our responsibility toward Him if He is loving and just.

I believe that God has created us to be like Him, only on a smaller scale, of course! He has made us to love each other, to care for His creation responsibly, and to be secure and confident in who we are. But our selfishness and emotional hurts hold us back from being the people our Father intended us to be.

The fact that God cares for us and offers us freedom from our selfishness and healing for our hurts is what has motivated my wife and our family to live in Amsterdam's red light district and share His love there. That is why we lived for three years in Afghanistan. It was there that we met Steve, who had a unique story to tell....

CONTENTS

1

*The Hurting Heart
of Man*

1

The Hurting Heart of Man

He called himself Steve, but I had the feeling this wasn't his real name. His jeans were old and bleached, not because he had bought them that way in a trendy European boutique, but because of constant wear on the "hippie trail." He had traveled overland from Amsterdam with a friend on the Magic Bus, a cheap but sometimes risky travel service, and they had recently come to Kabul, Afghanistan.

My wife, Sally, and I, along with a few stalwart friends, lived in Kabul and ran a free clinic for the Western society dropouts who drifted across Central Asia in search of adventure, drugs, and escape from the lifestyles they

11

had come to loathe. Many had been pushed to the fringes of society by rejection and a deep sense of alienation. Nothing in their surroundings provided a sense of identity or belonging. Steve was no exception.

In the weeks that followed, he occasionally visited us at the clinic. One day he surprised me by asking if I wanted to hear about the happiest day of his life. This was the first time he volunteered to talk about himself, so I was eager to listen.

"I'll tell you the happiest day of my life," he said as a strange smile spread across his face. The locked-in pain and hostility erupted in a torrent of anger.

"It was my eleventh birthday. That was the day both my parents were killed in a car accident!"

His voice seethed with bitterness. "They told me every day of my life that they hated me and didn't want me. My father resented me and my mother constantly reminded me that I had been an accident. They didn't want me, and I'm glad they're dead!"

In the weeks ahead I continued to try to help Steve, but lost track of him soon after that. His pain and anger, however, remain vividly etched in my memory.

What Sally and I discovered in Afghanistan in the early 1970's was not just a few wounded Westerners running away from their problems, but a whole subculture of hurting people. Over the past ten years we have invested our lives helping emotionally wounded people and have discovered that *no level of society* is immune from the pain of broken relationships.

One upper-class young man who came to us for counseling described how his father made him look on as he beat and stabbed his mother. A young woman told us of the humiliations and molestations she suffered at the hands of her father, brothers, and grandfather. Another young man confided in us that his parents gave him to his grandparents simply because they did not want him. His grandparents, in turn, put him in an orphanage at the age of five. There the director beat him every Sunday if he refused to go to church. Years later he committed his life to Christ through our work in Afghanistan, and then returned home to express his love and forgiveness to his parents with a gift. When his mother saw him, she cried out in rage and would not let him enter the house. A handsome young husband wept as he shared that he could never remember hearing the words "I love you" from his lawyer father.

Our world is plagued by an epidemic of pain. With divorce rampant and child abuse scream-ing from the national headlines, it is not sur-prising that for many people the concept of a *Father* God evokes responses of anger, resent-ment and rejection. Because they have not known a kind, caring earthly father, they have a distorted view of the heavenly Father's love. In many cases these hurting individuals choose to simply deny or ignore His existence.

John Smith, my friend from Melbourne, Australia, tells about talking to a hardened, street-wise teenager who gave him one chance to tell him about God.

"Okay, mate," he said, "what is God like?"

Fresh from theological studies, John blurted out, "He is like a father."

The young man's eyes blazed with hatred. "If he's anything like my old man, you can have Him!"

Later John learned from a social worker that the youth's father had raped his sister repeatedly and beaten his mother regularly.

Emotional Wounds

Negative childhood experience is not the only factor that can hold us back in our understanding of God as a Father. Many people experience an emotional or mental block when they try to call God "Father" because they do not know Him *personally*. There is a difference between knowing about God and knowing Him personally. John 1:12 says, "To all who received him, who believed in his name, he gave power to become children of God." To become a child of God, we must believe that Jesus Christ came as God's Son, died, and was resurrected so that our sins could be forgiven. We then need to ask Him to forgive us and to become the Lord of our lives. We need to dedicate our lives to learning and obeying God's Word, and worshiping Him alone.

Other people have difficulty relating to God as Father because they have been taught all their lives to respect Him, and to them that means addressing Him as "Thou." To use an informal term such as "Papa" or "Father" seems disrespectful to them. Yet the Bible teaches us to call God "Father" when we pray (Matthew 6:9), and that He wants to have a close, intimate relationship with us, His children.

Some of the most common hindrances to our comprehension of the Father heart of God are emotional wounds. These injuries often result in "scar tissue" which makes us hesitant to fully trust Him as our Father.

The Bible offers many examples of emotional injury, and refers to it as a "wounded" or "broken" spirit. The book of Proverbs says, "A glad heart makes a cheerful countenance, but by sorrow of heart the spirit is broken" (15:13). "A man's spirit will endure sickness, but a broken spirit who can bear?" (18:14).

The story of King Saul's daughter Michal clearly illustrates the pain of a "wounded" or "broken" spirit. Michal was raised in an environment charged with friction and conflict.

Her father, an impatient, insecure man, often exploded in fits of anger. No doubt she was deeply affected by his wrath.

Saul's jealousy of the future King David led him to devise a plot to kill him. As enticement, he offered one of his daughters as a prize to David if he could kill 100 of Israel's enemies, the Philistines. "Surely," thought Saul, "David will be killed by the Philistines and I can be rid of him forever!"

Much to Saul's dismay, David succeeded. In fact, he killed 200 Philistines! Saul awarded Michal as the "prize," but David soon fled from another of Saul's fits of anger and left her behind. Several years later he returned and found Michal married to another man. Against the will of her and her new husband, he demanded her return. She was eventually torn from the arms of her weeping husband and forcefully returned to David (2 Samuel 3:13-16).

It seems that Michal was moved between the men in her life like a pawn in a chess game. Given her upbringing, it is understandable that she reacted to David with such bitterness. Her resentment exploded at the height of a victory celebration.

"As the ark of the Lord came into the city of David, Michal the daughter of Saul looked out of the window, and saw King David leaping and dancing before the Lord; and she *despised* him in her heart.... And David returned to bless his household. But Michal the daughter of Saul came out to meet David, and said, 'How the king of Israel honored himself today, uncovering himself today before the eyes of his servants' maids, as one of the vulgar fellows shamelessly uncovers himself!'... And Michal the daughter of Saul had no child to the day of her death" (2 Samuel 6:16,20,23).

Michal's response flowed from an emotional wound which had festered into hatred. Forgiveness was the medicine that could have brought healing, but she chose not to grant it. Spiritual and physical barrenness afflicted her for the rest of her life.

There are many modern-day Michals, with varying degrees of pain, but they don't have to end up like she did. Because of His Father heart, God longs to renew and restore us through the healing power of His love.

His Heart

A dictionary definition of "heart" is "one's innermost being; the essential part." The Father heart of God describes that foundational element that characterizes who He is. Through His words in the Scriptures, Jesus described God as a merciful, forgiving, kind, and loving Father. Through His life He demonstrated our heavenly Father's very nature.

"What does God look like, Daddy?"

I can remember struggling one night several years ago with how to answer the question posed by my then five-year-old daughter, Misha.

As I pondered Misha's question, I realized that in her childlike simplicity she had asked a question that many people want answered. Perhaps adults state it differently, but the basic question is still the same. *If there is a God, what is He like?*

The Bible says that God is not a finite being like you and me, but He has made Himself known to us in such a clear, understandable way that we can know what He is like. "No one has ever seen God; *the only son*...he has made him known" (John 1:18).

I told my daughter what God looks like. *I told her that He looks like Jesus.* In fact, Jesus once said, "If you have seen me you have seen the Father" (John 14:9). Jesus is God in human form. We find many examples of how Jesus revealed the Father to us in the Bible. One example of this is found when some Jewish mothers wanted Jesus to bless their children, but His disciples thought He was too busy, too important to be bothered by these mothers. But Jesus scolded His disciples and told them to bring the children to Him. He took the children in His arms and talked to them. He had time for them, He had time to listen to their stories and hear about their games. He didn't mind getting dirty from little kids sitting on his lap, runny noses and all. Through seeing how Jesus had time for the little children, we learn that God has time for people. He cares, even about the little things in life. He is patient. *God the Father looks like His Son.*

On another afternoon Jesus stopped to talk to a Samaritan woman by a well. At that time Samaritans were hated and despised by the Jewish people. Women were considered second class citizens and incapable of comprehending spiritual truths.

Jesus elevated this woman to a place of equality and value by the mere fact that he broke social custom and spoke with her publicly. In doing so, He further revealed what God is like. By directly discussing this woman's spiritual needs with her, Jesus demonstrated His concern for her personally and also showed that God the Father cares for men and women equally.

Not only was this lady a Samaritan, but she was also an immoral woman. Jesus knew that, yet He was not ashamed to be seen with her. He actually *wanted* to talk with her. That is why he traveled through Samaria: to take time to show *real love* to this one who was known for her affairs with men. He saw past the outward hardness, the loud jokes, and the sarcasm about religion: He saw her heart; He saw her longing for something to fill her emptiness; He saw her need to feel loved, cared for, and special.

She in turn received His love because He had helped her "see" God in a way she had never seen Him before. That is why Jesus came: to reveal *God* to us, and to bring *us* to God.

2

A Perfect Father

2

A Perfect Father

I have often wondered why God chose to have us enter this world as helpless infants. He could have devised a reproductive system that produced physically complete persons like His "originals"—Adam and Eve. Instead, He opted to create us as beings in process, persons who would slowly grow physically, emotionally, and mentally, and eventually emerge as adults.

I believe that God designed us to begin our lives as babies, totally dependent and vulnerable, because He intended the family to be the setting in which His love was modeled. He desired that children grow up feeling understood, loved, and accepted. Nurtured in this kind of loving, secure environment, youngsters could develop a healthy, God-based self-esteem and see themselves as wanted, important, valuable, and good.

Unfortunately, many homes do not meet this ideal. Countless people have suffered hurt and rejection from their families and have had no real father figures with whom to identify. These experiences have kept them from knowing God as He really is and have hindered them from enjoying true intimacy with Him.

Following are seven different areas of misconception about God that frequently stem from childhood situations. For the sake of clarity, I will be referring almost exclusively to God's fatherlike qualities.

Authority

When the family dog greets you as you drive up to a friend's house, you can sometimes tell a lot about the way it's been treated. The typical dog either cowers away and trembles with fear or else showers you with an unwanted display of affection demonstrated with tongue, tail, and dirty paws! The browbeaten puppy that cannot be persuaded to trust you has probably been mistreated. The exuberant critter that surprises you with a tongue-lap facial has likely come from a loving home. We often approach God in a similar way. Our past experiences color our responses when He reaches out to us. What breeds distrust in the area of authority?

A bedroom door bursts open. A small boy is slapped awake in the middle of the night by a drunk and angry man. The terrified child screams as the dark, hulking shape of a man he calls "Daddy" beats him mercilessly.

A 15-year-old prostitute stares with blank, empty eyes as she mechanically endures another night of degradation. She doesn't care what happens to her. She hasn't felt clean since the night she was molested by her own father.

We, like the browbeaten puppy, sometimes shrink away from the authority of our Father God because we assume He will be like the other authority figures in our lives. He will not. He is perfect love. It is He who commands, "Parents, don't keep on scolding and nagging your children, making them angry and resentful. Rather, bring them up with the loving discipline the Lord himself approves" (Ephesians 6:4 TLB).

Trust

As a child you may have never known a father because of death or divorce. Maybe you were "orphaned" by the demands of your parents' careers. Now, as God's child, it is hard for you not to doubt His faithfulness. You can't erase the childhood memories of broken promises and neglect. Perhaps you only rarely sense His presence and tend to approach Him with cynicism and distrust.

Yet your heavenly Father was there when you first walked as a child. He was there through the hurts and disappointments of your teen years, and He is present at this moment. You were briefly loaned to human parents who, for a few years, were supposed to have showered you with love like His love. The care and security of a good home and family was intended by God to prepare you for His love. If your family failed in that responsibility, you need to recognize that fact, forgive them, and go on to receive God's love. He waits even now with outstretched arms.

God is the *only* Father who will never fail us. As 2 Timothy 2:13 says, "Even when we are too weak to have any faith left, he remains faithful to us...and he will always carry out his promises to us" (TLB).

Values

A few years ago a friend visiting a native village in the South Pacific spent some time watching the children play. These children, he told me later, seldom heard the words, "Don't touch that! Leave it alone! Be careful!" Their homes were simple, consisting of earth floors, thatched roofs, and mats that rolled down to serve as walls at night.

In contrast, our modern homes are stuffed with expensive and fragile furnishings and appliances that represent a minefield of potential rejection for inquisitive toddlers. How many mothers have exploded in anger at a child over a shattered vase or antique! Children constantly hear about the importance and value of *things*. Very few times, however, do they hear the simple words, "I love *you*."

A repetitious and destructive chant is working its way into the subconscious minds of our children: "*Things* are more important than *me*. *Things* are more important than *me*!" I am not suggesting that we abandon our homes, but we do need to realize that our concept of God's generosity may have been crippled by our childhood experiences. We may need to radically alter our priorities so we can communicate God's love to our children.

God's values significantly differ from ours. Creation displays an extravagance of color, complexity, and design that goes far beyond simple *functional* value. A tiny white flower kissed by the sunlight in the Italian Alps has meaning to God even if it is never seen by a human eye. It may not hold economic value, but it was created by God in the hope that one day one of His children might glance at it and be blessed by its beauty.

The greatest demonstration of God's Father

heart is revealed in His attention to the details of our lives. He longs to surprise us with the "extras," those little pleasures and treasures that only a father would know we desire. God is not stingy, possessive, or materialistic. *We* often use people as things; *He* uses things to bless people. And He manifests His generosity through more important gifts than just material goods. He freely gives us the priceless intangibles of forgiveness, mercy, and love.

Affection

When my small son comes in from the backyard covered with mud, I pick him up and wash him off with the garden hose. I reject the mud, but *not the boy*. Yes, we have sinned. Yes, we have broken God's heart. But we are still the center of His affections—the apple of His eye. It is *He* who pursues *us* with forgiveness and love. We say, "I found the Lord," but the truth is that He found us after much pursuing.

Many children, particularly boys, receive very little physical affection from their fathers, and no real compassion when they hurt. Because of our society's false concept of masculinity they are told, "Don't cry, son; boys don't cry." God's love, however, heals the hurts of men and women alike. As our Father, He feels our pain more deeply than we do because His sensitivity to suffering is so much greater.

Most of us have probably tried to forget the painful moments of our lives, but God has not. He has perfect recall. He was there when you experienced cruel teasing on the school playground and you walked home alone, avoiding the eyes of the other kids. He was there when you sat in that math class confused and dejected. When you got lost at the age of four and wandered terrified through the crowd, it was He who moved the heart of that kind lady who helped you find your mother. "I led them with cords of human kindness, with ties of love" (Hosea 11:4 NIV).

Sometimes we don't understand what a loving Father God really is. Your parents may proudly display your pictures in an album, but how does that compare with His infinite capacity to be overjoyed with your every success? God heard you speak your first real word. He watched with delight as you spent hours alone exploring new textures with baby hands. He treasures the memories of your childhood laughter. There has never been another child like you, and there never will be.

Moses once invoked a blessing on each of the tribes of Israel. To one he said, "The beloved of the Lord...makes his dwelling between his shoulders" (Deuteronomy 33:12). That is where *you* dwell also. Whatever you become in the eyes of men—even a person of great authority, fame, or title—you will never cease to be more or less than a child in the arms of God.

Presence

There is one attribute of God that not even the best parent can hope to imitate—His ability to be with you all the time. Human parents simply cannot give their children attention 24 hours a day. But God is different. Not only is He with you all the time, but He gives you His undivided attention: "Let Him have all your worries and cares, for He is *always* thinking about you and watching everything that concerns you" (1 Peter 5:7 TLB).

Your parents were often preoccupied with their activities and uninterested in the minor events of your life. God, however, is not that way. He is a God of detail. The Bible says that He has even numbered the hairs on your head. Why? Not because He is so concerned about abstract mathematics; this biblical illustration simply paints a picture of how well He knows us and how much He cares about our lives.

A little boy worked all afternoon pounding nails into pieces of scrap wood. He finally emerged from the garage and showed a three-level battleship to Mom. He couldn't wait until Dad got home. Dad was late. But at 6:30 a tired, preoccupied man finally arrived. A cold dinner was waiting, as were more repairs to do on the house. The excited boy proudly displayed his handiwork to a daddy who barely looked up from his calculator. Daddy never looked, but God did. He always looked, always took delight in the work of the little boy's hands.

God is our real Father, and always will be. Try not to resent the failings of your human parents, for they were just kids who grew up and had kids themselves. Rather rejoice in the wonderful love of your Father God.

Acceptance

We live in a performance-oriented society. Many parents convey the message that *if* you make the football team, *if* you bring home a good report card, *if* you look pretty, *then* you are accepted and "loved." God, however, is a God of *unconditional* love. Our heavenly Father loves us because *He is love*. Although we don't need to do anything to convince Him to love us, we do need to *receive* His love. This does not mean we have to become saints first. All He asks is that we come to Him honestly and sincerely; then He will forgive us and make us His children.

Many people have difficulty accepting God's love and approval. A true love relationship, however, involves the giving and receiving of love. Imagine how I would feel if I impulsively decided to surprise my wife with some flowers, but when I handed them to her and said, "I love you, Sally," she ran to get some money to pay for them! I would be hurt and disappointed. All I really want to know is that she feels the same way about me.

What is your response to God when He says He loves you no matter what? Can you receive His love without rushing into frantic activity to earn His approval?

One of the greatest pictures of contentment is that of a baby asleep in the arms of his mother after having been fed at her breast. The child no longer squirms and demands, but rests in the loving embrace. A deep sense of peace wells up into the sound of a lullaby sung by mothers at times like this. In the Bible, the prophet Zephaniah described a similar emotion in the heart of God for us: "He is mighty to save, he will take great delight in you, he will quiet you with his love, he will rejoice over you with singing" (Zephaniah 3:17 NIV).

Your Father loves you just as you are. All through life you have had to perform and compete. Even as a tiny baby you were compared with other babies. People said you were "too fat" or "too thin" or had "his legs" or "her nose." But God delighted in your uniqueness, and He still does.

Communication

Open, loving communication is difficult for many parents, especially for fathers. Yet God clearly communicates His love to us. In fact, He loves us so much "that he gave his only begotten son, that whosoever believeth in him should not perish but have everlasting life" (John 3:16 KJV).

One girl told me she couldn't talk to God. She felt like her words were thudding into a brick wall. She could not remember God ever answering her prayers. As we prayed together she realized that she pictured God as if He were her own father, good and honest but quiet and shy. He was a man who had rarely spoken to his children and never told them he loved them. When she admitted that her father had been weak and had even failed her, she was able to forgive him and accept him as he was. This recognition opened up a whole new dimension in her relationship with God. She had more faith to pray because she realized He did hear her. She soon sensed God's guidance and presence in her life.

If you believe that you have been hindered in your relationship to God because of a lack in some area of parental love, then tell the Lord how you feel and ask for His help. You *must* choose to forgive anyone who has hurt you. If you don't, bitterness will consume you, and you will find no peace with God.

Also realize that you are not alone. I haven't met a perfect person yet, or a parent who hasn't made mistakes. Everyone has suffered some kind of hurts in his or her life. What counts is that you get to know God for who He really is—and our concept of Him is often quite different from reality.

God is the Perfect Parent. He always disciplines in love. He is faithful, generous, kind, and just, and He longs to spend time with you. Your Father wants you to receive His love and to *know* that you are special and unique in His eyes.

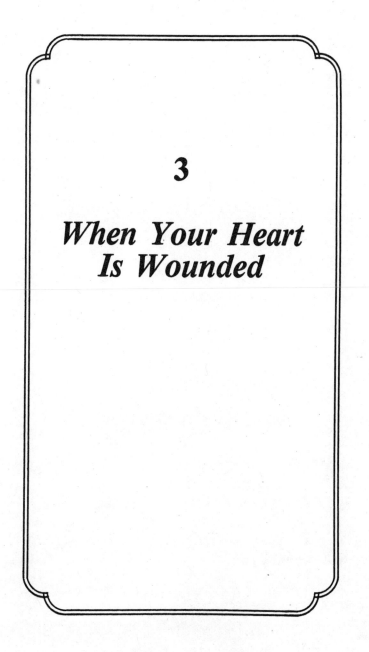

3

*When Your Heart
Is Wounded*

3

When Your Heart Is Wounded

She was shy, and a bit taller than most teenagers. I was tired. The last thing I wanted to do was talk to a self-conscious teenage girl. I had just finished teaching a group of South African people about God's Father heart, and I desperately wanted to rest. Yet I sensed I should listen carefully to what she was about to say.

Her question seemed almost pointless at first, but then I began to wonder if she really wanted to tell me something more. I waited. When she finished, I asked her if there wasn't something else she wanted to share. She looked relieved. She sat down beside me in the small, crowded auditorium and whispered in my ear, "Can I cry on your shoulder?" "Sure," I said, "but can you tell me why?"

Her eyes brimmed with tears as the story came out. Her father had died when she was very young. Since that time she had had nobody's shoulder to cry on, no daddy to talk to about her questions, disappointments, achievements, and plans. A dull ache throbbed in her heart as she desperately missed those big, loving arms that once held and comforted her.

She cried unashamedly on my shoulder, then we talked to our Father in heaven. Together we asked Him to heal the hurt and fill the empty space in her life.

And He did. I saw the same girl a few years later when I was back in South Africa. I did not recognize her at first, but when she reminded me of the special time of prayer the memories came flooding back. She thanked me for the moments we had shared and told me they had made all the difference. In our short time together she *experienced the Father heart of God.*

This young woman had suffered from a deep emotional wound which had kept her from fully enjoying her relationship with her heavenly Father. Our world is full of people with these invisible injuries, many resulting from childhood, but many also inflicted by the pressures and problems of modern life. God our Father desires to heal these hurts in order to insure sweet and genuine fellowship with His children.

The Bible speaks specifically about the need for healing of damaged emotions and depicts this as part of the sanctification process. In the Old Testament book of Isaiah, the writer points to the future time when God will send a Savior to rescue people from their sin and selfishness. He describes the Savior as "a man of sorrows and acquainted with grief" (53:3). He goes on to say that "He has borne our griefs and carried our sorrows," and that "by His stripes we are healed."

This healing is for both the guilt of our selfishness and the *consequences* of our selfishness—the scars and the wounds we bear in our personalities and emotions. In Isaiah 61 the writer says that this Savior will "bring good tidings to the afflicted... [and] bind up the brokenhearted...proclaim liberty to the captives and the opening of the prison to those who are bound" (v. 1). Those who mourn will be given the "oil of gladness" (v. 3). In Psalm 34:18 David says that the Lord "is near to the brokenhearted and saves the crushed in spirit." In Psalm 147:3 he says that the Lord "heals the brokenhearted and binds up their wounds." *This is good news for a broken world.*

In spite of all that God offers us, many people still picture Him as sitting up in heaven, removed from the pain and harsh reality of this fallen world. "Why has He created us and then left us to ourselves?" they question bitterly.

But God is not the cause of our problems, and He has not left us alone in our suffering. He came and lived among us. He became a man. He endured all that we have gone through and much more.

He created man, but man rejected Him. He sent messengers and prophets to remind His people that He was their Creator, but they stoned the prophets and killed the messengers. So finally God sent Jesus to reveal Himself. The Creator stepped into His creation, but the creatures refused to recognize Him. In fact, they crucified Christ on a cross. What did the Creator do then? He transformed this greatest of mankind's cruelties and made it the source of man's forgiveness! *We killed Him but He used the act of our greatest selfishness to be the source of our forgiveness.*

Jesus Christ is the wounded Healer. He knows how our emotions can be injured. Indeed, He was tempted in every way that we have been tempted.

His very birth was questioned, and His mother's reputation was slandered. He was born in poverty. His race was ostracized and His hometown ridiculed. His father died when He was young and in His latter years Jesus traveled the streets and cities homeless. He was misunderstood in His ministry, and abandoned in death. He did all this for you and me. He did it to identify with us in weakness: "We have not a high priest who is unable to sympathize with our weaknesses, but one who in every respect has been tempted as we are, yet without sin. Let us then with confidence draw near to the throne of grace, that we may receive mercy and find grace to help in time of need" (Hebrews 4:15,16).

God the Father sent Jesus Christ into the world to bridge our separation from Him. Separation resulting from our selfishness is at the core of many emotional wounds. If left untreated, it often develops into what I call the "Saul Syndrome," which leads to alienation from God and other people. Jesus came to introduce reconciliation in place of alienation, healing in place of woundedness, and wholeness in place of brokenness.

The Saul Syndrome

He was a tall, striking man. The reddish tint of his hair and well-trimmed beard added to his stature and dignity. He carried himself with regal bearing; all eyes followed him when he passed through a crowd.

He had the ability to draw men to himself, rally them to a cause, and inspire them to greatness. The people had no fear of entrusting him with their secret dreams and hopes. He was a leader's leader.

Or so they thought.

Underneath the broad shoulders of this tall, magnificent-looking leader lay a heart that brooded with jealousy and fear. So deep were his insecurities, so uncertain the foundations of his personality, that he perceived any hint of greatness in others around him as a serious threat to his own position in the nation.

Most of his followers were so enthralled with his ability to mobilize and communicate that they didn't notice his fanatic desire to have *total* control. A few perceptive men, however, began to have their doubts.

His brilliance in battle strategy and uncanny ability to take the right step at the right time convinced distant followers of his greatness, but only confused those close to him. "He must be the Lord's anointed," they thought. "He always seems to be right." They did not want to admit the obvious: his violation of principle, his lack of servanthood, his unwillingness to promote others, his anger and impatience—all of which seemed to disqualify him from being king. In fact, they were deeply embarrassed and ashamed of his secret rages of anger and his fits of melancholy and depression.

Finally there was one man who was no longer

confused about the character of this king: the prophet Samuel, who had anointed him into office.

In a simple act of obedience the prophet had poured oil on the king's head and prayed over him, and in so doing had installed a man to rule a nation. Unlike many other men, Samuel was not impressed with his own "power." He had learned from early childhood that there is only one acceptable response to the voice of God: simple, childlike obedience.

Now Samuel's heart also raged within him, not in uncontrolled anger, but in righteous indignation. Enough was enough. He had waited patiently, watching the internal destruction of the kingdom due to the king's lack of integrity and obedience. He saw the deep insecurities of the king, the painful striving to find worth and security in the praise of his fellows. He had agonized over this man countless nights in prayer and weeping. He had fasted many days, asking God to change the king's attitude and to help him find his security in the Lord's approval. But it was to no avail.

Now the word of the Lord came to the prophet: "I repent that I have made Saul king; for he has turned back from following me, and has not performed my commandments" (1 Samuel 15:11).

In a few moments of terrible confrontation it was done: The king's authority was taken from him. He remained in office, but that was no guarantee of authority. Power can come from a position, but authority comes from character, obedience, and God's anointing.

A closer study of the life of Saul reveals a pattern—a terrible, unmistakable cycle of inferiority and emotional hurt...the "Saul Syndrome."

First Samuel 15:17 says that Saul was "little in his own eyes." This is not to be mistaken with true humility, for if that had been the meaning of Samuel's words, there would have been no need to remove Saul from the throne. Samuel was saying that even though Saul felt inferior and looked down on himself, he was still responsible for all his actions before God. Feelings of inferiority never excuse disobedience.

First Samuel 15 lists the characteristics of Saul's personality: *stubbornness and independence* ("Rebellion is as the sin of divination, and stubbornness is as iniquity and idolatry"), *pride* ("Saul came to Carmel, and behold, he set up a monument for himself"), *fear of man* ("I have sinned because I feared the people and obeyed their voice"), and *disobedience* ("Why then did you not obey the voice of the Lord? To obey is better than sacrifice"). Simply illustrated, the Saul Syndrome looks like this:

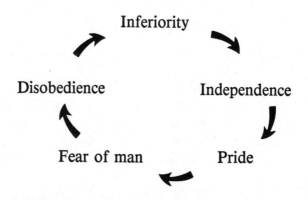

One problem leads to another. If we do not deal with our emotional hurts in God's way, they will lead us to independence from God, which in turn produces pride. Pride is much more concerned about what people think of us than what God thinks of us, which results in the fear of man. The fear of man inevitably leads to disobedience. We may still do a lot for God, but we are practicing a religion of dead works.

Some of the most wounded people I know are also some of the most proud and independent. Emotional injury makes us extremely susceptible to this vicious syndrome and no one is immune from it.

To help identify the Saul Syndrome, I have described some of the characteristics that often appear in our daily lives.

1. *Withdrawal or isolation.* The Saul Syndrome leads us to cut ourselves off from other people. Withdrawal can be a way of covering up or justifying our refusal to forgive those who

have hurt us, or to compromise with those with whom we disagree.

2. *Possessiveness.* The mentality of "my ministry," "my group," "my opinion," "my job," or "my place in the church" is selfish and stems from an attitude of independence. The Bible teaches that rebellion is as the sin of divination; it comes from hell (1 Samuel 15:23). This "me-first attitude" is sin.

3. *"Us-versus-them" mentality.* When we are caught up in the Saul Syndrome we start thinking in terms of "us" and "them," those with whom we agree versus those with whom we disagree. This thought pattern signals that we are not just disagreeing but are judging other people and creating factions in the church.

4. *Manipulation.* Proud and independent people can be manipulative by refusing to cooperate, demanding their own way, criticizing, or constantly judging what others are doing. We spiritualize our reasons, of course, and that is why our manipulation can be all the more dangerous.

5. *Unteachableness.* The Saul Syndrome causes us to be closed to other people. We refuse to accept correction and instruction. We become very hardened.

6. *Critical and judgmental attitude.* We justify this in many ways, but it all boils down to slander and judging the motives of others.

7. *Impatience.* We think our way is better,

and refuse to wait for others who don't agree or understand.

8. *Distrust*. The Saul Syndrome results in distrust. We accuse others of not trusting us, but that is often a projection of our own mistrust. It reflects our independence and has more to do with our needs than the needs of others.

9. *Disloyalty*. This involves playing on the doubts, wounds, or needs of other people to win them over to our own point of view rather than seeking to build unity, love, forgiveness, and reconciliation.

10. *Ingratitude*. We focus on what we think should be done for us instead of how much has already been done for us.

11. *Unhealthy idealism*. We idolize a method, standard, or program and put it above people, particularly people with whom we disagree. Ideals become more important than unity or correct attitudes.

Even though the Saul Syndrome is often a symptom of hurt and unresolved feelings of rejection, it is still selfish and wrong and must be dealt with ruthlessly. *There is no problem of independence and inferiority that cannot be solved through greater humility and brokenness in our lives.*

The Bible promises that as we humble ourselves, God will give us grace (James 4:6,7). We are afraid of "humiliation," but that is not what the Bible means when it says to humble ourselves. True humility involves *the willingness to be known for who we really are and to take God's side against our own sin.* Most people respect us *more*, not less, for humbling ourselves and confessing our needs. I believe that God *always* does.

If you are caught up in the Saul Syndrome, may I suggest that you will never be free from it until you accept your responsibility to repent of these wrong attitudes. It will do no good to blame other people for your own problems or to make excuses for your own sin. Humble yourself before God and others. Cry out to Him in earnest prayer.

Many years ago I saw this pattern in my own life. I ached with deep insecurities, yet was also very proud and independent. I longed for acceptance and affirmation but would not confess my desperate need for help. I was obsessed with what other people thought of me, particularly other leaders. It was only when I humbled myself before others and repented before God that He delivered me from the Saul Syndrome. I vowed to God that I wanted Him to deal with these problems in my life more than I wanted leadership, attention, or acceptance from others. I call it my "Joseph Covenant." I spent time alone with God one day in a forest in Holland and cried out to Him. I told the Father that I wanted Him, *at any cost*, to root out independence, pride, and fear of man from my life. I told Him that I would wait as long as it took for this to happen, even 12 years like Joseph in Egypt, and that I did not want to take any shortcuts in getting my life right with Him. That was a costly prayer, but I have never regretted it. God heard me that day and made some significant changes in my life.

Freedom from the Fear of Man

We will never be truly free to love our Father God if we are dominated by the fear of man. The Bible says that the fear of man is a snare, a trap. We become prisoners of fear, always worried about what others think, dominated by the actions of others instead of the Word of God. Do you feel that you're always looking over your shoulder, trying to figure out why you're not included or worrying about what other people are saying about you? Are you determining your actions by how much approval they will bring from other people rather from pleasing God? If so, you are bound by the fear of man.

The remedy for the fear of man is the fear of God! The fear of God is not an emotional fear or a fear of God's wrath. The Bible defines the fear of God very specifically:

1. *The fear of God is hatred of sin.* Proverbs 8:13 says, "The fear of the Lord is hatred of evil."

2. *Friendship and intimacy with God are equated with the fear of the Lord*. Psalm 97:10 says, "The Lord loves those who hate evil," and Psalm 25:14 says, "The friendship of the Lord is for those who fear him."

3. *The fear of the Lord is deep respect and awe of God*. Psalm 33:8 says, "Let all the earth fear the Lord, let all the inhabitants of the world stand in awe of him!"

4. *The fear of the Lord is the beginning of wisdom and knowledge*. Proverbs 1:7 says, "The fear of the Lord is the beginning of knowledge."

The fear of the Lord is not evidenced by some kind of holy look on your face, nor is it heard in some sort of quivering tone in your voice when you pray. It is not revealed in the way you dress or in the great number of rules you obey.

Having the fear of the Lord simply means to love God so much that you hate all that He hates. This kind of hatred is not born out of religious neurosis, nor is it a reflection of our culture. It comes from being so close to God, so in tune with His character, that we love what He loves and abhor what He abhors. The fear of the Lord is not a crusading anger, it is anger over *the destructiveness of sin*. It sees the cruelty, the deceptiveness, the oppressiveness, and the destructive force of sin, and hates it for what it is.

The fear of the Lord does not come into our

lives by accident. It indwells us because we choose to seek it (Proverbs 1:28,29; 2:1-5) and make it top priority of our life. It comes because we get sick and tired of being manipulated and controlled by the fear of man, of being dominated by our fears and insecurities. It comes because we cry for it, pursue it, and get desperate for it.

The Saul Syndrome can be broken. *You can be free*, but there is a price to pay. If you want to experience inner healing and to know the Father's love, then you must choose the fear of the Lord. Proverbs 14:26 says, "In the fear of the Lord one has strong confidence." It is humility and the fear of the Lord that bring us close to the Father heart of God and lead us into wholeness and self-worth.

How God Heals Wounded Hearts

In the next chapter I have listed the steps to the healing of emotional and psychological wounds. I have not intended for these steps to be treated as some sort of magic formula or talisman to wave in God's face. The truths that each one of these steps represents must be applied to our lives as we are ready for them, with the guidance of God's Spirit. (If you don't know how to be guided by God's Spirit, ask Him to help you. He has promised to help all those who ask Him.) Take each step and apply it personally to your situation.

If your problems are complex, you may need the help of a professional counselor or psychologist. In the back of this book is an Appendix with guidelines on how to choose professional counselors or psychologists. You have a right to ask them questions before you allow them to ask you questions. You should never submit yourself to being helped or counseled by someone unless you are secure with the person and confident that he is skilled and competent.

We don't have to live in permanent emotional pain. Because of our heavenly Father's love for us and because Jesus has suffered in our place, we don't have to carry our wounds with us all our life. We can be healed and set free to live in the joy of His love. We must, however, be willing to pay the price.

4

Healing from a Loving Father

4

Healing from a Loving Father

I once met a man in Madras, India, who said he had never sinned! Because of our mutual interest in religion, our casual conversation quickly turned to serious matters. When I shared that I believed God forgave those who acknowledged their sin, he asserted that he had never done anything wrong.

"You've never lied?" I asked him.

"No, never," came the answer.

"You mean you've never stolen something or hated someone?"

"No, not even once."

"Have you committed adultery?"

"No."

"Disobeyed your parents?"

"No."

"Did you ever cheat on an exam in school?"

"No, not that either."

I was baffled. Then I thought of another question. "Are you proud of the fact that you have never sinned?" I asked mischievously.

"Oh yes," he replied, "Very proud, very proud!"

"There you are," I said, "Your first sin. You are a proud man!" He then laughed loudly and congratulated me that I had caught him in his only sin!

Though we are not all as proud as this man, we have all followed in Adam's original sin. Adam denied God's right to rule over his life, and he chose to go his own way. We have all made the same decision. It is hard for us to admit that we too have rebelled against God and denied His right to be Lord of our lives.

Without acknowledging this most basic of human problems—our selfishness—dealing with the wounds and unmet needs in our lives only postpones the inevitable. Painkillers cannot keep a terminally ill cancer patient alive. They relieve the pain, and that is important, but why settle for a temporary solution if there is a permanent cure for the cancer?

As a loving Father, God longs to forgive us if we will only acknowledge our pride and selfishness and ask Him to forgive us. He wants us to have a deep relationship with Him, and desires to remove any hindrances to our communication with Him.

Some people feel that because His Word calls us sinners, God is rejecting us. That is not the case at all. He is simply helping us to understand the most basic problem we have and how to overcome it.

However, we are not only sinners. We are also *sinned against*. Either intentionally through their selfishness or unintentionally because none of us is perfect, other people do things to us that hurt us deeply. Being sinned against does not excuse wrong responses on our part, but it helps us understand ourselves and others who struggle to respond in the right way when we have been mistreated or hurt.

To gain the maximum healing and blessing, I suggest that you go through the following steps slowly and prayerfully. Take time after reading each step to pray and apply it to your life. If it becomes too painful, ask a friend or spiritual leader to go through the steps with you. You need to be prepared for pain if there are unhealed wounds. In order for them to heal properly, they may need to be opened and cleansed of any "infection" or bitterness that has set in. Even though this is painful for a time, it will bring great joy and healing in the long run. It will liberate you to draw even closer to the Father heart of God.

How God Heals Our Emotional Wounds

Step One: Acknowledge Your Need of Healing

For most people this is not a problem. Yet if we are wounded and we do not acknowledge our need, there is little opportunity for healing or help in our lives. Being able to admit our need is a sign of good mental health, as well as evidence of self-honesty.

All of us need healing and growth in our emotions and personalities. *Don't feel that you are an exception.* It is an attitude of teachableness and humility that will allow the healing to begin in your life. Some of us struggle with exposing our need because of fear of rejection. But the opposite is true: When we admit our needs, other people respect us more for our honesty. All of us can probably recall a time when we made ourselves vulnerable and then were hurt by someone who did not respond to us in love or wisdom. But we can't let those experiences keep us from the healing that God wants to give. Past rejections shouldn't be allowed to determine our actions or attitudes for the future.

Start by being honest with *God.* He knows you intimately and He won't reject you. In fact, He is longing and waiting for you to be honest so you can receive His love and help. Tell Him your hurts, fears, disappointments—everything.

Next, open up to someone who can help you

work through these steps of healing. Choose a *trusted* Christian friend who will pray with you and encourage you.

If you have wronged others, you will need to go to them and make it right. This is a part of acknowledging our needs. We do this not *in order to be forgiven by God*, but *because we have been forgiven*. The fruit of being in a right relationship with God is wanting to have broken relationships with other people restored as well.

John Stott, the famous Anglican theologian, gives some very valuable cautions regarding this area in his book *Confess Your Sins*. He talks about the circle of open confession: secret sins, private sins, and public sins. He says we should confess sins only on the level that they were committed. If it is a secret sin—that is, a sin of the heart or mind that was never acted or spoken out to others—then it needs to be confessed only to God. There is freedom to share these things with close friends or fellow Christians out of a desire to be honest and accountable, but we don't have to do that. That is our choice. In fact, we should do it only when we feel secure with others and when we feel that God is specifically leading us to do so—never because we feel pressured. Even then, we must be wise and careful about how we share.

It could be very unwise to confess some sins of the heart to other people. If the person you sinned against in your mind doesn't know about it, don't burden him or her with it unless there is a clear reason why it will be helpful. If you are in doubt, don't do it until you can seek mature counsel.

There are some sins that are done in the secret or private level of our lives that are "shameful" in nature. I believe we need to see a restoration of a sense of "shame," particularly over sins of sexual impurity. If we must ask someone to forgive us for sinning against him or her in this way, we should not go into details or be unwise in our words. Say what needs to be said. Confess that you have failed him or sinned against him, and ask his forgiveness. That is enough.

A good guideline to follow is that if it is a secret sin, confess it to God; if it is a private sin, ask forgiveness of the one you have sinned against; if it is a public sin, ask the group's forgiveness.

To summarize, the steps to healing and wholeness as related to honesty about our needs are:

> A.   Admit your needs and sins. Honesty releases God's grace in our lives.
>
> B.   Receive God's grace. Grace is God's gift of love, acceptance, and forgiveness to us, and it makes us secure in Him. That security builds faith.

C. Trust the Lord and others. Faith results in trust and makes it possible for us to have close relationships with God and people.

D. Build heart-to-heart relationships with God and others. These relationships are made possible when we have humbled ourselves. God can then channel love and forgiveness to us personally and in our hearts toward others.

The opposite of this process leads to further pain and emotional injury:

A. Broken relationships. When relationships are broken, we find it very difficult to trust other people.

B. Legalism. When our relationships with other people are wrong, we tend to become judgmental and critical. We live by "law," not God's grace. This causes us to mistrust others.

C. Mistrust. When we don't trust others, we often exude that mistrust, and they in turn don't trust us. An atmosphere of rejection grows, and walls grow up between us and others.

D. Walls. Walls produce separation, the very opposite of heart-to-heart relationships.

In looking at being honest about our needs, it is important to distinguish between a sin, a wound, and a bondage. For sin there needs to be forgiveness, for a wound there needs to be healing, and for spiritual bondage we need to be set free. Sometimes we need help in all three areas.

You cannot confess a wound as if it were a sin, because a wound is not a sin. Yet if as a result of being hurt you have developed a sinful attitude or response, even if others are to blame, *God still holds you responsible for your response.* In fact, God does not see it as a matter of the other person being 80 percent to blame and you 20 percent; *both you and the other person are 100 percent responsible for your own actions.* Until you accept total responsibility for your own attitudes and actions, healing is hindered. Why is that? If your attitude is one of resentment, bitterness, or an unforgiving attitude, God's healing and forgiveness are blocked. "For if you forgive men their trespasses, your heavenly Father also will forgive you; but if you do not forgive men their trespasses, neither will your Father forgive your trespasses" (Matthew 6:14,15).

I cannot overstress the importance of acknowledging our need of healing in our lives. I have seen many people busy doing things for God, but their activity was tainted by their need to prove themselves, gain acceptance, or overcome insecurity about what they were doing. Our service to God and to other people should flow out of our security and sense of well-being, not out of a drive to prove ourselves or out of a need to "be somebody." In the long run we will be able to grow closer to our loving Father, we will feel better about ourselves, we will enjoy our work more, and we will be a greater blessing to other people if we take time to receive wholeness and inner healing.

Step Two: Confess Your Negative Emotions

Some of us go through life collecting negative emotions. Many of us were not taught how to identify or communicate our feelings, so we have stored anger, disappointment, fear, bitterness, guilt, and other negative feelings since early childhood. Suppressing one emotion on top of another is like pushing one layer after another of garbage into a plastic rubbish bag. Something finally has to give. This process of building up unidentified and uncommunicated emotions produces tragic consequences, ranging from ulcers to suicide. Many of us haven't learned how to cope with difficulties. We are physically grown but emotionally stunted. We harbor emotional barriers to giving and receiving in our relationships with others and with our Father.

Dr. Phil Blakely notes that to deal with this problem we need to "decompact," to talk out the emotions built up inside us. To do this, it is important to have someone who can help us get our feelings out. For Christians, that should begin with prayer. If Jesus is not the One we turn to before and above all others, we will never be healed. He is our Creator; He longs for us to share our feelings with Him because He cares so deeply for us.

Then we need to talk to other people as well. It is important to develop friendships with people who let us be ourselves, but who love us enough to challenge us when we are wrong.

Airing our emotions is not a panacea in itself. Communication of feelings simply clears our mental channels so the root causes of our problems can be dealt with. If we share stored-up feelings of guilt, this does not mean we have dealt with the causes of the guilt. This is where relativistic psychology breaks down. To get people talking about their guilt feelings can make them feel better, but if one does not eventually accept responsibility for violating God's moral laws, the feelings of guilt will return (unless, of course, a person completely sears his or her conscience and loses the ability to feel at all).

Though emotions in themselves are not necessarily sinful, they can result in sinful responses if they are directed in a negative way toward God, ourselves, or other people. That is where we need biblical standards to gauge whether our attitudes have become sinful. If they have, we must treat them as both *unhealthy* and *wrong*.

God does not intend for us to live *by* or *for* our feelings. Some people live by the axiom that what they *feel* is good *is* good, and what they *feel* is bad *is* bad. That is good existentialism, but not biblical Christianity. We are to live according to the truth revealed in the Bible, not the whims dictated by our feelings. God has given us the capacity for emotions, and He intended them to be an encouragement for making right choices. When we do not live by God's laws, then we have a tendency to twist God's original intentions for emotions and use them to reinforce a lifestyle of pleasure and selfishness. Some people are totally ruled by their emotions, while others don't even know they have deeper feelings. They have suppressed their feelings to the point where they think it is very "Christian" not to show emotion at all. This is not being mature or "spiritual." God created us to live a balanced life in which we express and enjoy our emotions and are free to deal with them honestly and constructively.

Husbands, fathers, and spiritual leaders can be a great help by encouraging their families and congregations to share their feelings freely. Our desire to lead others can be ineffective or even harmful if those we lead are not given that privilege. By creating room for those around us to be honest we can lead them into a deeper relationship with God. They will trust us more and will sense our commitment to them, which in turn will give us the freedom to speak candidly into their lives.

Where there is no trust, we have no authority. By giving people the opportunity to be honest, we are "giving grace." This in turn gives them the security to be honest not only about their emotions, but also about their needs. If those we are leading exhibit a serious mistrust of other people, especially authority figures, it could be that they have never learned to express their feelings honestly in an atmosphere of love and acceptance.

One afternoon my wife Sally was sharing her frustrations about some personal problems. I immediately began to give her advice. I'll never forget her response: "I didn't come to you for you to preach to me. I *know* what I need to do. When you preach to me, it makes me feel like you're not listening or caring. *I need someone to listen to me. If I can't talk with you, who can I go to?*" I decided that day that I wanted to be the kind of husband who gave the freedom and security to my wife (and to others, for that matter) to share feelings with me without fear of judgment, sermonizing, or reprisal.

To break the cycle of emotional suppression and mistrust, ask God to give you the opportunity to talk with an authority figure who encourages you to be honest about your feelings.

Also, forgive those in the past who have not given you the freedom to do so. Your motive in sharing how you feel should not be to persuade that person of your point of view, but to be honest. Honesty, however, is not an end in itself. Your honesty should proceed out of a desire to confess negative emotions so that you can become the person God wants you to be.

If we have been hurt by authority figures or disagree with them, it is our responsibility to pray first before we confront them. If after praying we still don't understand a decision they have made, then we should ask them to clarify their point of view. We can feel free to disagree with a leader, but we must be careful not to let that disagreement affect our attitude toward him or her. We can disagree without becoming judgmental or breaking fellowship. Disunity never takes place because of disagreement. Constructive disagreement is healthy. It is when disagreement gives way to criticism or judgment that division can occur. *Every problem of unity can be solved with greater humility or forgiveness.* God is concerned about our *heart attitude* as well as about helping us grow by being open and honest about our feelings.

Step Three: Forgive Those Who Have Hurt You

Forgiveness is not merely forgetting a wrong that someone has committed against us, nor is it a mystical kind of spiritual feeling. It is simply *pardoning a person for the wrong he has done.* It is giving our love and acceptance in spite of being hurt.

Forgiveness often involves a process, and it is seldom a one-time act. We keep on forgiving until the pain goes away. The deeper the wound, the greater the forgiveness. Just as a doctor has to keep our physical wounds free of infection so they can heal properly, so we must keep our emotional wounds clean of bitterness so they too can heal. Forgiveness is the antiseptic for our emotional wounds. As often as you think of a particular person and feel hurt, forgive him. Tell the Lord that you forgive the person and that you choose to love him or her with His love. Receive His love for the person by faith. Do that each time you think of the person until you feel you have truly forgiven him or her.

God's forgiveness toward us should be our motivation to forgive. If you find it difficult to forgive someone else, think about how much God has forgiven *you*. If it does not seem like a lot, then ask Him for a revelation of your life as He sees it. He will answer your prayer if you cry out to Him sincerely.

Step Four: Receive Forgiveness

If you have been hurt by other people and have sinned in your reactions to them, it is important not only to forgive the ones who hurt you, but also to ask God for forgiveness for your wrong actions toward them. As you do this, you may discover a need to forgive yourself. At times our greatest enemy is our own sense of failure. We can often be much harder on ourselves than on anyone else. If you have failed, pour out your sense of failure to the Lord in prayer, confess your sin, and tell Him that you receive His forgiveness and that you forgive yourself. Each time you feel that sense of failure returning, thank the Lord for His forgiveness.

There is a difference between conviction of sin and condemnation. Condemnation stems from a sense of failure. Conviction results from sin. Conviction is specific, clear, and from God; condemnation is vague, general, and from ourselves or Satan. If you think you have sinned, but are not sure, ask God for conviction. As a loving Father, He will discipline you. If conviction does not come as you wait before Him in prayer, thank Him for His love and forgiveness and go on with your day. Remain open to Him showing you wrong attitudes, but do not become paralyzed by introspection. Do not wallow in the pigpen of self-pity. It is too destructive.

If you have wrong attitudes toward anyone who has hurt you, it is crucial that you confess them to God. Be careful, however, because self-pity can be a counterfeit for real repentance. Dealing with our role in the matter often releases God's Spirit to work in the hearts of other people. Even if this does not happen, it is still our responsibility to keep our lives right before God. If you become critical, hard-hearted, jealous, independent, proud, judgmental, or bitter, *then you need to deal with your responses*. As you are humble before God, He will forgive you and give you healing for your own wounds. *There is healing through forgiveness!*

Step Five: Receive the Father's Love

There is a void in our lives that can be filled only by God Himself. When you sin and ask for forgiveness, or you struggle with insecurity or inferiority, there is the possibility that this void is not full. Ask God at those times to fill you to overflowing with His Spirit. Stand against self-centeredness by keeping your focus on Him. I cannot overstress the importance of this step in the healing process. *Self-pity and self-centeredness grieve the Holy Spirit*.

Concentrate your thoughts and prayers on God's character and on different aspects of His Father heart. Worship Him: Speak to Him, sing to Him, and think about Him. Meditate on His faithfulness, His holiness, His purity, His compassion, His mercy, and His forgiveness.

Developing an attitude of worship is a vital part of receiving the Father's love. Cultivate this trait above all others. Memorize Scriptures or songs that you can use as weapons to combat loneliness or discouragement. Worship is the doorway that leads into the Father's presence and away from depression and self-pity. Some people say they cannot worship God when they don't *feel* like it because they think that would be hypocritical. My answer is that we don't worship God because of how we feel, but because of *who He is*. I often worship God *in spite of my feelings*. I don't want to be a prisoner of my feelings, so I praise God anyway. If I'm discouraged, I try to honestly express those feelings, but then I go on to focus on *who He is*, not on how I feel.

Do you want to receive the Father's love? Then spend time in His presence. We are bathed in His love as we spend time with Him, giving to Him. What can we give Him? Through our words and thoughts we can offer Him honor, adoration, attention, praise, and worship. If this is difficult for you, go through your Bible and underline the passages that specifically speak about the character of God. The book of Psalms is a good place to begin. Then pray and sing those passages to the Father in your times of prayer. As you do this daily, you will find yourself growing more and more in love with Him. You will sense His presence intimately near you in response to your words of praise. Do not be surprised when He speaks words of appreciation, approval, and love throughout the day. He loves to love His children!

Step Six: Think God's Thoughts

In response to the wrongs we suffer, especially as children, we build destructive habits of thinking about ourselves. For example, if your parents were demanding and perfectionistic, you probably often failed to live up to their expectations. People with this kind of upbringing often "program themselves" for failure. By determining beforehand that they will fail, they try to protect themselves from disappointment. Unfortunately, such expectations are often self-fulfilling. These negative thought patterns are rarely accurate or kind, and are based on fear or rejection. If we think we are ugly, we will not only feel that way but will act that way as well.

The Scriptures say that we should love God with all our heart, soul, mind, and body, and that we should love our neighbor *as ourselves* (Leviticus 19:18; Matthew 19:19). God wants us to love ourselves, not selfishly, but with His love. He wants us to think His thoughts about ourselves—thoughts of kindness, esteem, respect, and trust.

If you think in negative thought patterns about yourself, I suggest that you stop right now and write down the two or three negative ways of thinking that are most common for you. After you have done this, write down God's thoughts toward you, based upon His character, that are the opposite of the negative thoughts.

For example, if you wrote down that you think you will always fail, write "I am good at _____," naming one thing you do well. Also write down what the Bible says about that area of your life. For example, "I can do all things through Christ who strengthens me" (Philippians 4:13 NKJV). *Every time you start to think the negative thought, stop and say the positive thought, along with a Scripture.* It takes three weeks to break a bad habit and replace it with a good one. Keep telling yourself the truth until you have broken the negative thought pattern.

Don't give in to lies and condemning thoughts. Persevere—with God's help you can do it! Cry out to Him each time you fail; then start again. Have you ever noticed in the Bible how often God repeated a truth when He was trying to encourage someone? In the first chapter of Joshua He told Joshua *four* times not to be afraid. Why? Because Joshua needed to be reminded to think God's thoughts about himself. He was getting ready to go into battle and needed that encouragement. I'm sure he must have repeated those words of the Lord over and over to himself.

The most common cause of depression is thinking depreciating and condemning thoughts about ourselves. To break this cycle of depression, we need to follow the steps I have outlined and then *get sick and tired of being tired and sick*! We need to break the habit of negative thinking by thinking God's thoughts.

This same principle also applies to reactions that go beyond thoughts to actions. As you become aware of certain "reaction patterns" in your life that are negative, defensive, or selfish, write them down. Beside them, write down how God wants you to react in the situations that cause you to be threatened or defensive. When you find yourself acting in a negative or selfish way, stop and pray; then choose the way God wants you to respond.

Ask God to enable you to put these thoughts and choices into action. When you fail, ask for His forgiveness and keep going. If the devil tells you you have "failed again," agree with him, but tell him you refuse to feel sorry for yourself! Accept responsibility for your failure, ask God's forgiveness or help, and *go on*! Keep working at it until you have established new habits. It took years to develop the negative ones, so don't give up because it takes a few weeks or months to replace them with God's patterns. Start with one or two habits at a time, and then go on to others. As we do the possible, God will do the impossible for us.

Step Seven: Endure

Ninety percent of success is finishing! The Bible says, "If we endure, we shall also reign with him" (2 Timothy 2:12). Endurance has two aspects: On the one hand, it means a commitment on our part to not give up, a determination to finish. On the other hand, it has to do with God's enablement. God gives us the grace to accomplish what He calls us to do. His commands are also His promise of victory.

Sometimes you might feel that it is impossible to endure to the end. That may be right! But when we come to the end of what is possible for us, then we can see God do the impossible. Faith has not begun until we believe God for the impossible. We don't need faith to do what is possible. So if you are facing impossible situations in your life, praise God, for now you can begin to exercise your faith.

Why is endurance a step in God's healing process in our lives? Giving up is what makes us vulnerable to feelings of resentment, anger, hurt, rejection, lust, mistrust, or whatever may be plaguing us. Sometimes we want God to perform a miracle and take away all our problems *right now*. Our Father, however, is leading us through a process that is preparing us to reign with Him in heaven. Because He wants to mold and refine us, He allows us to experience temptations which *force* us to make choices.

As my friend Joy Dawson says, "It's how you finish that counts!" The apostle Paul says in his first letter to the Corinthian church, "Do you not know that in a race all the runners compete, but only one receives the prize? So run that you may obtain it. Every athlete exercises self-control in all things. They do it to receive a perishable wreath, but we an imperishable. Well, I do not run aimlessly, I do not box as one beating the air, but I pommel my body and subdue it, lest after preaching to others I myself should be disqualified" (1 Corinthians 9:24-27).

We will fail along the way, but as we confess our sins, turn away from them, and choose by faith to hate them, we receive God's forgiveness and a new beginning. *He is the God of new beginnings.* Our part is to humble ourselves and turn away from our sin or failure; His part is to forgive us and give us a new start. He loves to do that, because He is our Father and He is a God of love.

He is at work in you. *The struggle is part of the victorious healing process.* You are learning invaluable lessons: humility, forgiveness, compassion, and endurance. Press on. We are in a war, but we are on the winning side! Jesus is the Victor! "I am sure that he who *began* a good work in you will *bring it to completion* at the day of Jesus Christ" (Philippians 1:6).

God is seeking to find the people who will fulfill His original intentions when He created mankind. *He wants friendship with us.* And He does not just want this with a collection of selfish individuals; His purpose is to unite in a family all those who love Him. So whenever people love God, He draws them together to enjoy deep friendship, mutual care and support, and celebration of the love and forgiveness and wholeness that He has given them. These "family units" are what the church is intended to be.

The Father's Family

Besides the steps we can take as individuals, the "Father's family" is also a channel of His love and healing to wounded people. As we love and accept and forgive one another as brothers and sisters in Christ, God's love flows through us to heal one another. Through our brothers and sisters in God's family, God provides the kind of love and acceptance that frees us from our fears and allows us to experience greater wholeness as people. We can be committed to others without fear of rejection. We can accept others in spite of their weaknesses. We can forgive others even when they hurt us. We can be ourselves without fear of rejection. All of this is true because of God's grace. It is His grace, His undeserved love, that does this for us. We don't have the ability in ourselves to be so loving, but God enables us to love. We don't have the ability in ourselves to heal one another, but through us God heals others. Every Christian has this ministry. Each of us can be a "grace-giver."

At this point it is important to bring a gentle

warning. If we are wounded, we should be careful not to put our focus on people as the *source* of healing in our lives. People cannot give what only God can give. *If you want people to heal you, you will easily be disappointed.* Get your attention on the heavenly Father; He is the only one capable of totally healing you. He will often do that *through people*, but He is the source and people are the channel.

Emotional healing is almost always a process. It takes time. There is an important reason for this: *Our Heavenly Father does not merely want to free us from the pain of past wounds.* He also desires to bring us into maturity, both spiritually and emotionally. This takes time and right choices. He loves us enough to take the months and years necessary to not only heal our wounds but also build our character.

Without growth of character we will get wounded again. We will commit foolish, selfish acts that will hurt us or provoke other people to hurt us. Because God loves us, He waits for us to want this kind of character growth; He waits for us to be ready to be healed. Often our right responses to other people release healing in our own lives.

5

The Heart of Disappointment

5

The Heart of Disappointment

Excitement pulsed throughout Jerusalem that day. After many years of civil war, the nation was once again united, its enemies to the south defeated. Most important of all, after 20 long years of spiritual barrenness, worship was being restored in the new capital of the united kingdom. Saul's rule had ended with his death in the battlefield, and now young David was the leader. It had been a long night, and the dawn was finally breaking.

David had declared to the nation that he was returning the ark of the Lord to Jerusalem. Tens of thousands of people gathered in the city to celebrate. Every family and tribe was represented, and the throngs of people were alive with expectation.

"Surely God is pleased," David must have thought to himself. "Now His people are united and we can worship the Lord once again. Yet how grievous," he reflected, "that Saul did not honor the Lord by bringing back the ark of God. But this is not a time for sadness. I too will rejoice before the Lord."

And David and all the house of Israel were making merry before the Lord with all their might, with songs and lyres and harps and tambourines and castanets and cymbals (2 Samuel 6:5).

Suddenly tragedy struck. The oxen stumbled and young Uzzah put out his hand to steady the ark. He instantly fell to the ground dead! David was stunned. What did this mean? Silence fell over the people as word of what happened spread through the crowd.

Anger, embarrassment, and fear descended simultaneously on David. "Why, Lord?" he pleaded, "Why now? I am doing what you have commanded. Why Uzzah? He only touched the ark."

Though David was confused, he knew he could not proceed with the ark until he knew why God had judged his actions. Disappointment overwhelmed him. If only he knew why...what had he done to displease the Lord?

Can you imagine the sadness David experienced as he walked home alone that day? It had started off to be such a beautiful occasion. No doubt he wrestled with feelings of personal failure and condemnation, while at the same time struggling with the anger he felt toward God.

And David was angry because the Lord had broken forth upon Uzzah; and that place is called Perez-uzzah to this day. And David was afraid of the Lord that day; and he said, "How can the ark of the Lord come to me?" (2 Samuel 6:8,9).

Most of us can identify with David's feelings. We too, at one time or another, have stepped out in faith and have faced disappointment and tough times. "Why?" is the question we ask again and again.

Disappointment can also result from other people's responses to us. They can let us down when we need them most, and they often fail to meet our expectations.

Whatever the cause, disappointment brings the potential for hurt, discouragement, bitterness, anger, unbelief, and fear. The effects of extreme disappointments can linger with us for months or years, hindering our relationship with our Father God. That is why it is so important to learn to deal with disappointment constructively, and to see His purpose in allowing us to experience it.

In his book *Don't Waste Your Sorrows*, Paul Billheimer points out that our disappointments can be a source of great blessing if we respond to them in the right way. Nothing can injure us emotionally unless it causes us to respond with the wrong attitude. Disappointing circumstances will pass, but one's reaction to them determines a moral and spiritual choice which can influence one's life forever.

As long as there are people, there will be disappointments. A friend of mine once said, "We're going to have unity around here even if I'm the only one left!" Coming to terms with disappointment involves learning to deal with people's weaknesses. It requires us to develop patience, flexibility, and a deeper understanding of God's ways. We need to learn to respond as God would have us to in every circumstance. This does not mean that we become human doormats, but it does mean that we respond with a Christlike attitude no matter how we are treated.

Learning to Eat in Peace

Christians learning to love and accept one another are much like brothers and sisters learning to eat dinner together in peace. I can remember fuming at my sister and brother during family dinnertime, but I also remember that bickering at the table was something my father would not tolerate! He insisted that we learn to eat together in harmony.

Some of our disappointments stem from our

unrealistic expectations for each other. Becoming a Christian does not mean instant perfection. We need to *learn* to love our brothers and sisters, just as we have to learn to "eat in peace."

When you are disappointed in the actions of a brother or sister, don't "turn him off" or cut him off from further fellowship. God may have brought him into your life to teach you valuable lessons. The psalmist David said, "In faithfulness thou hast afflicted me" (Psalm 119:75).

People whom we see as difficult may be a loving "affliction" from the Lord. If you and I were as loving as we often think we are, we would have no trouble in responding to "hard-to-love" people. I believe that God allows, sometimes even arranges, trying experiences in our lives to expose our character weaknesses and wrong attitudes so that He can deal with them.

Overcoming Pride

King David was forced to deal with disappointment when Uzzah lost his life, and it required a great act of humility on David's part. He could have hardened his heart in pride and blamed God for what had happened. Instead, he sought God to find out what he had done wrong, and what lesson God had for him. David learned to humble himself in order to discover God's purpose in those tragic circumstances.

Humility means not only being honest but adopting God's perspective. Many people are ruthlessly honest, but they don't go on to take God's side against sin and embrace His attitude toward the sinner. Both are necessary if we are to learn from the disappointments of life.

For people who learn to ask God why He allowed a situation to take place or what He wants to teach them through it, disappointments produce tremendous growth and heightened spiritual understanding. On the other hand, pride presents the greatest barrier to learning through difficulty and disappointment. Although we would think that sympathy is our greatest need during times of disappointment, I believe our urgent need is to recognize our pride. Overcoming pride is the key to gaining victory and understanding when we are disappointed. Consider these symptoms and how they can hinder us in responding in the right way:

Pride sees the wrongs of others but never identifies with their weaknesses. When others fail we can respond, "Yes, I've done that too," or, "I understand; if it were not for God's grace I would have done that also."

Pride does not usually admit wrong or personal responsibility. When it does, it excuses it or explains it away, and there is no sorrow for the wrong done.

Pride blames others, criticizing and pointing out why *they* are wrong.

Pride produces hardness, arrogance, self-sufficiency, and unhealthy independence.

Pride is more interested in being accepted in the eyes of other people than in being right according to God's standards.

Pride is more concerned with winning arguments than with keeping friends.

Pride never says the words, "I am wrong. It is my fault. Will you forgive me?"

Pride breeds a demanding attitude. It focuses on what *has not* been done for us rather than on what *has* been done for us. It covets the past or the future, but is never satisfied with the present.

Pride is divisive. Pride says that "my" group or church or denomination has more truth than others.

Pride causes a person to judge situations by what they mean to man and not to God. Pride does not look for God's perspective.

Pride gossips, tears down, ruins reputations, and delights in spreading news of failure and sin.

Pride blames God and other people when things go wrong.

Pride excuses bitterness and resentment.

Pride leads to pity and pity and more pity.

Pride says that a person can reach a level or depth of spirituality in which we are finally free of pride. It puts its security in a grotesque form of self-righteousness, and not in the cross of Jesus Christ.

It was in the most painful, disappointing

experience of my life that I learned about pride: my own pride, and the pride of others.

I had heard of divisions within the church and deep, tearing conflicts between people, but it never entered my mind to think that it would happen to me.

In our body of believers we had put an emphasis on relationships and unity, on being a "family" loving one another, and I was proud of the fact that we were on the "cutting edge" of the church. When I looked at other groups, I was often disgusted at their superficiality and lack of personal warmth, although I wouldn't have admitted it at the time. I could not imagine being publicly identified with some parts of the body of Christ because of their apathetic approach to evangelism or their lack of radical discipleship.

I taught on priorities in the body of Christ and stressed a lifestyle that was worthy of the Kingdom of God. I felt strongly about the church being a *community* of believers, and the importance of the highest quality of relationships. I still teach on these things, but ten years ago I taught them to such an extreme that Jesus was no longer the center of my life—other believers were.

We were a community of people who had become infatuated with ourselves. We saw ourselves as unique, and when that happened we were in for big problems.

We had set such high standards for ourselves,

that not only was it impossible for other believers to live up to them—we couldn't either.

Eventually we turned on each other. Christmas Day 1975 was the saddest day of my life. I found myself sitting on my bed that morning and contemplating my shattered dreams. I had dreamt of a loving community of people living the gospel so radically that we would shake the world, but I had neglected to calculate the fallenness of man into my equation for success. So dreadful was our failure, so hurt was I by my own sin and the sin of others, that I despaired of life itself.

I cannot describe the pain. I felt crushed, rejected, betrayed, and at times angry at the very people I loved so much. Our little paradise of love and healing had turned into a hell of broken relationships. I was faced with the brutal reality of who we had become when God's grace was not controlling our lives.

I look back on those terrible, dark months with great thankfulness to God. It was the most painful period of my life—and the best. God did more in those days of division and shattered dreams to show me myself, my deep insecurities, and my pride than I had seen in the rest of my life put together. Correspondingly, He showed me more of His mercy, love, and faithfulness at that time than I ever dreamed possible.

Because of the pain that I experienced in those days, and the healing and redemption that came as I humbled myself before God and others, I learned many lessons. When the breakthrough finally came in my own life, God revealed to me the root of my own wrong attitudes toward others. I wept as I heard Him gently whisper into my mind, "I forgive you, and I restore to you all that has been lost."

It was that experience that gave me a greater awareness of the danger of pride, and a deep tenderness for those who have experienced hurt and disappointment in their relationships with others.

David humbled himself again and again. The Bible says that he was a "man after God's own heart." It was David who wrote in Psalm 51, "The sacrifice acceptable to God is a broken spirit; a broken and contrite heart, O God, thou wilt not despise" (v. 17).

To David, brokenness did not mean despair or hopelessness or being hurt. It was humility, the opposite of pride. Because of that, David learned from every disappointment in life. His psalms of praise flowed out of the crucible of life's disappointments.

If we want to learn to trust God and know Him as our Father, as David did, we need to humble ourselves before Him. When things go wrong, we can either look for God's reasons or become hard and proud. There is no middle ground. A mixture of humility and pride will not bring the results that God desires. Even if we have done nothing wrong in a situation, we still need to learn to forgive and bless our enemies. That can only happen when we have humble hearts.

Below are some simple questions I have learned to ask myself which have proved to be invaluable in dealing with disappointment.

1. Lord, what do You want to teach me in this situation? What attitude should I have? What should be my response? What biblical principles, if any, have I violated in this situation?

2. Has there been any disobedience on my part regarding the action, the timing, the people involved, or the method?

3. Lord, do I need to forgive anyone in this disappointment?

4. Do I need to seek the counsel of any godly person for help in this situation? Would You please give him or her the kind of insight into my life, my needs, and my reactions that will help me to learn what You want me to learn?

5. Lord, am I overspiritualizing this situation and missing some practical lessons I should learn?

6. Lord, what are the adjustments and changes I need to make? Help me to take the necessary steps so I can get on with life.

7. Who should I now be serving, instead of worrying about myself?

It is sometimes hard to "internalize" the lessons of life. If we were raised without the example of godly parents of without wise, loving discipline, applying lessons learned from disappointments or difficulties can be difficult and threatening. If that is the case, you may tend to feel rejected, dominated by "heavy-handed" authority, or fearful when a situation is really intended by God to help you grow. You may need assistance to help you understand how to grow and learn from disappointment. *Healing for Damaged Emotions* and *Putting Away Childish Things*, both by David Seamands, are excellent resources in this area, and I highly recommend them.

When Jesus knelt alone to talk with the Father on that fateful night in the Garden of Gethsemane, His heart was heavy. He faced the ultimate trial—death. His Father had asked a hard thing of Him, but He was not forced to act against His will. He accepted His Father's plan because He knew and trusted Him.

Christ said, "Not my will but Thine be done." Because He knew God's heart, He obeyed Him unconditionally. It was not a forced response to an overbearing Father, but a trusting response to known love.

How we deal with disappointment and respond to what God wants to do in our lives reveals, perhaps more clearly than anything else, how secure we feel in His love and how close we are to His Father heart.

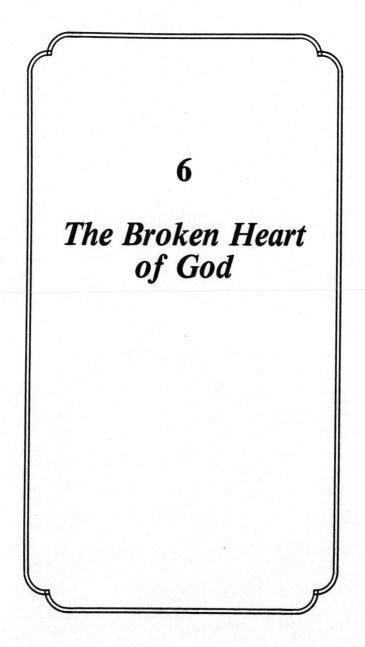

6

*The Broken Heart
of God*

6

The Broken Heart of God

After a long week of lecturing and counseling in Norway, I was "people-tired." I love my work, but by the end of six 18-hour days I just wanted to be alone.

As I climbed out of the taxi in front of Oslo's International Airport, I sent a silent prayer heavenward. My request was simple enough: All I wanted was a seat on the airplane to myself with a little extra legroom (for my six-foot-plus frame) so I could spread out and rest on the three-hour flight back to Amsterdam.

I walked down the center aisle of the plane, slightly stooped over to avoid hitting my head on the ceiling. I found an empty row of seats by a bulkhead, so that meant extra legroom and a quiet flight back to the airport. I smiled to myself smugly as I settled into the aisle seat, thinking how good God had been to answer my prayer for a little rest and peace. "God understands how tired I am," I mused.

As I placed my briefcase under the seat in front of me, a smiling, rather disheveled man sauntered up the aisle and greeted me boisterously: "Hi! You an American?"

"Yes...yes I am," I said weakly. I had taken the aisle seat thinking it would have been harder for anyone to sit by me, since he would have to step over my long legs! The man sat down in the row behind me, but I paid him no heed and began to read.

After a few minutes his head came around the corner.

"Whatcha reading?" he asked as he peered over my shoulder.

"My Bible," I replied a bit impatiently. Couldn't he see I wanted some solitude? I settled back in my seat, but a few minutes later I felt the same pair of eyes looking over my shoulder. "What kind of work do you do?" he asked.

Not wanting to get involved in a long conversation, I answered briefly, "A kind of social work," hoping he would not be interested. It bothered me a little that my statement wasn't quite accurate, but I dared not tell him I was involved in helping needy people in the inner city of Amsterdam. That surely would provoke more questions.

"Mind if I sit by you?" he asked as he stepped over my crossed legs. He seemed oblivious to my efforts to avoid him. He reeked of alcohol and spit as he spoke, sending a fine spray all over my face.

The man's obnoxiousness incensed me. His insensitivity had destroyed all my plans for a quiet morning. "Oh, God," I groaned inwardly, "please help me."

The conversation moved slowly at first. I answered a few questions about our work in Amsterdam. I began to wonder why this man so desperately wanted to talk to me. As the conversation unfolded, I realized that I was the insensitive one.

"My wife was like you," he said after a while. "She prayed with our children, sang to them, took them to church. In fact," he continued quietly, his eyes misting over, "she was the only real friend I ever had."

"Had?" I asked. "Why do you refer to her that way?"

"She's gone." By this time the tears were beginning to trickle down his cheeks. "She died three months ago giving birth to our fifth child. Why," he gasped, "why did your God take my wife away? She was so *good*. Why not me? Why her? And now the government says

I'm not fit to care for my own children. They're gone too!"

I took his hand and we wept together. How selfish I had been! I was only thinking of my need for a little rest when this man desperately needed help.

He went on to tell me that after his wife died a government-appointed social worker recommended that the children be cared for by the state. He was so overwhelmed by grief that he couldn't work and he also lost his job. In just a few weeks he had lost his wife, his children, and his work. With the holidays just a few weeks away he couldn't bear the thought of being home alone at Christmas. Now he was literally trying to drown his sorrows.

He was almost too bitter to be comforted. He had grown up with four different stepfathers and had never known his real dad. All of them were harsh men. When I mentioned God, he lashed out, "God?" he said. "I think if there is a God He is a cruel monster. How could a loving God do this to me?"

As I continued to talk with that wounded, hurting man, I was reminded again that many people in our world have no understanding of a God who is a loving Father. To speak of a loving Father God only evokes pain and anger within them. To speak of the Father heart of God to these people, without empathizing with their pain, verges on cruelty.

The only way I could befriend that man on the trip from Oslo to Amsterdam was *to be* God's love to him. I didn't try to give pat answers. I just let him be angry and then offered him the oil of compassion for his wounds. He wanted to believe in God, but deep inside his sense of justice had been violated. He needed someone to say it was okay to be angry and to tell him that God was angry about injustice too. By the time I had listened and cared and cried with him, he was ready to hear me say that God was more hurt than he was by what had happened to his wife and family.

No one had ever told him that God too knows the pain of a broken heart.

He listened in silence as I explained that God's creation, so marred by sin and selfishness, is completely different now from how He created it. He then asked the question that all of us ask: Why? Why did God create something that could become fallen and marred? If He is a loving Father, why does He allow all that suffering?

I then shared with him some answers that have helped me.

Many people cannot comprehend that a good God can exist and allow suffering. Yet if there is no personal-infinite God, *suffering loses all meaning*. If there is no God, man is just a complex product of time and chance—just the result of the evolutionary process. If that is true, then suffering is only a physical-chemical problem. If there is no God, there are no moral absolutes and therefore no basis to determine that any form of suffering is morally wrong. By denying His existence, men and women deny the ultimate meaning to life itself and therefore deny the basis of saying it is wrong for people to suffer. Without God, they could not even ask "Why do the innocent suffer?" because there would be no such thing as innocence. Innocence implies guilt, and guilt implies that some things are absolutely, morally wrong.

I believe that suffering is wrong, and the fact that God does exist allows me to say that emphatically. This assertion, however, leads to another important consideration—how God feels about suffering and evil in His creation. The Bible says that it brings great sorrow to His heart.

"The Lord saw that the wickedness of man was great in the earth, and that every imagination of the thoughts of his heart was only evil continually. And the Lord was sorry that he had made man on the earth, and it grieved him to his heart" (Genesis 6:5,6).

It is easy to ask questions concerning the justice of God, but if we are to live as His children and know His Father heart, we must examine *our response* to evil and suffering. Do we react as deeply as God does to evil in the world, to evil in our own lives? Do we share the sorrow of God's heart over sin and the destruction it brings to all that it touches?

I believe we can never experience complete healing for our emotional wounds or fully receive the Father's love unless we share God's sorrow over sin and selfishness. The Bible teaches that there is a difference between godly sorrow and worldly sorrow over sin. Paul wrote to the Corinthian Christians, "I rejoice, not because you were grieved, but because you were grieved into repenting, for you felt a godly grief, so that you suffered no loss through us. For godly grief produces a repentance that leads to salvation and brings no regret, but worldly grief produces death" (2 Corinthians 7:9,10).

Repentance involves not just being sorry, but being sorry enough to quit. Godly sorrow requires more than just confessing our sins. If we confess our sins but keep practicing them, we have not really experienced godly grief. Nor does repentance entail just feeling bad about what we have done. Sometimes we feel bad if we get caught, or we feel bad if we have to stop sinning, but godly sorrow is not dependent on feelings or selfish motives. Godly sorrow is based on *how sin hurts God and other people*. Godly sorrow produces a change in our attitude toward sin itself. We begin to hate sin and love goodness.

Godly sorrow also results in a new respect for God and His laws. His laws are very reasonable when you think about them: Do not kill, do not steal, do not lie, do not take other people's husbands or wives, and so on. To obey these laws is simply to live the way we were created to live. Cars were "created" to drive on roads, not through canals, over rockfields, or off the sides of mountains. They were made to be powered by gasoline, not water or Coca Cola. So it is with us. God created us to love one another, to be kind, unselfish, forgiving, honest, loyal to our husbands and wives, and to recognize and live in fellowship with Him. The very meaning of our existence is found in loving and obeying God. When we love God, a desire to obey His laws will come naturally. We should not strive to obey God's laws only so we can go to heaven, escape going to hell, be well-respected, or get something from Him. We should obey God's laws because He loves us and because we want to respond to His love by pleasing Him with our words and actions. Obedience should be a *love response* to God.

In Amsterdam there are laws against a man beating his wife. I do not beat my wife, nor do I need a policeman following me around with a gun at my back, saying, "I'm right behind you so you better not beat your wife!" Why don't I beat my wife? Is it fear of the law that motivates me? No! It is *love*.

Sharing God's broken heart also frees us to hate what He hates without feeling that we have lost our integrity. Many people hate God because of religion. They have associated Him with all the junk and hypocrisy they have seen in the church, and they have rejected *Him* as well.

Ninety percent of all agnostics have given up on God because of the false image of God or Christ which they have received through disillusioning encounters with the church or in other personal experiences. I think the Australians are a classic example of this. Some people, even some Aussies themselves, will tell you that most Aussies couldn't care less about God. But I don't believe that. Aussies have not rejected God; they have rejected *false images* of Him. The god they reject I reject also.

My Australian friend John Smith said in a university mission lecture that there are three false images of God that Australians have rejected, thinking they have rejected the God of the Bible:

1. The God of indifference
2. The God of privilege and prosperity
3. The God of arbitrary judgment

While early settlers emigrated to America because of their convictions, Australians were sent to Australia from England *for* their convictions, some for as little as stealing a loaf of bread. Australia was seen as a giant penal colony, and many of the prison wardens were priests and ministers. Imagine how most men felt about God if they were sent unjustly to an

Australian prison only to have their sentence enforced by a priest or minister. As John Smith says, "Australia has a history that causes many not to believe in God, when really they should not believe in man!"

If you have been offended by hypocrisy in the church, or if you have rejected an arbitrary God who gives men impossible laws and then sends them to hell for not keeping them, or if you are angry about injustice and poverty and have been presented with a God who does not care, then you can start over again without losing your integrity. You have not rejected the God of the Bible. You have not rejected Jesus Christ!

The God who has revealed Himself in Jesus Christ hates hypocrisy and injustice. The difference between God and us is not anger over injustice but the fact that He is absolutely just and we are not.

People like the man I met on the airplane get angry at God because they are hurt, either through personal disappointment or through reaction to injustice in the world around them. But a humble, honest man cannot permanently take out his anger on God because he must eventually acknowledge his own sin.

We have all committed, to some degree, the sins of the greatest criminals of history. We don't like to view ourselves that way, but in word or thought (and sometimes in deed) we express the same responses we judge in others.

We condemn Hitler ruthlessly, but are we just as ruthless in dealing with hatred in our own hearts? "I don't hate the Jews," we may say. But do we despise someone else—a neighbor, a co-worker, or a relative? If we have ever *hated* anyone, we have espoused the same attitude that motivated Hitler.

The proud man keeps on accusing God because he refuses to admit his own guilt. To deal with the problem of evil in the world, we must begin with ourselves. If we don't accept our own responsibility, we will eventually reject God's explanation for good and evil and come up with a philosophy that excuses us from acknowledging His right to rule in our lives. If we believe in God but still accuse Him of being unjust, we have never seen how our selfishness has brought grief to His heart.

Our sin has broken God's heart. God, however, has not just grieved over sin; He has done something about it. He gave His own Son as a sacrifice to pay for the sins of the world. We deserved to be punished for breaking God's laws, but He sent Jesus to take our punishment.

Most of us suffer, to some extent from a low self-image or emotional wounds, and there is a great temptation to become a self-centered person. It is easy to spend a lot of time feeling sorry for ourselves or thinking about our needs. Because of this, it is important to honestly face the dangers of this kind of self-centeredness and choose to put God at the center of our lives. We must choose to be more concerned about the pain that God feels in His heart over man's selfishness than about the hurts we feel. By deciding to put God first in our lives, we can break out of the patterns of manipulation, self-pity, or fear that plague us. God the Father yearns to love us as His children and heal us of our hurts, but that cannot happen unless we give Him full control of our lives.

Repentance and Receiving

If my children want to experience my love after they have done something wrong, they cannot do that by ignoring their wrong actions or taking my forgiveness for granted. Because I love them, I want to make sure their "I'm sorry" is sincere. I long to put my arms around them and hold them, but I love them enough to lead them to true repentance. If they have been disobedient or selfish, I take time to make sure they understand what they have done and why it is wrong, and then help them respond appropriately. When they acknowledge their misdeeds and express genuine sorrow, then my love can be *received*. I give it regardless, but I have learned that when they feel guilty for doing something they know is wrong, they are not free to receive and enjoy my love and acceptance.

Many times we sin because we are hurt, but that does not excuse us. To approach our reactions within a rationalizing psychological framework will not produce character growth in our lives. Even if other people have wronged us, we must deal with *our own* attitudes and actions. To receive the Father's love we need to accept responsibility for what we have done, said, or thought, and to ask God for forgiveness. When we know we are wrong, we must allow God to do His work in our hearts. We cannot gloss over sin, no matter how small we think it is.

Doing our part in this way makes it possible for us to receive the Father's love in full measure. We cannot heal ourselves, but we can acknowledge our wrong in a situation so that our focus is shifted away from blaming others or justifying or pitying ourselves. When we do this, our attention naturally centers on God. Then everything else can be right.

A little boy tore out a picture of the world from a Christian magazine, cut it up in smaller pieces, and then tried to put it back together. Finally he tearfully came to his father because he couldn't put the world together. The father had lovingly watched his son, and he knew that on the other side of the picture of the world was a picture of Jesus. Then he helped the little boy turn over each piece, leaving it in its same location, and explained to his puzzled son that when Jesus is in the right place, we *can* "put the world together again."

7

The Waiting Father

7

The Waiting Father

Sawat had disgraced his family and dishonored his father's name. He had come to Bangkok to escape the dullness of village life. He had found excitement, and while he prospered in his sordid lifestyle he had found popularity as well.

When he first arrived, he had visited a hotel unlike any he had ever seen. Every room had a window facing into the hallway, and in every room sat a girl. The older ones smiled and laughed. Others, just 12 or 13 years old or younger, looked nervous, even frightened.

That visit began Sawat's venture into Bangkok's world of prostitution. It began innocently enough, but he was quickly caught like a small

111

piece of wood in a raging river. Its force was too powerful and swift for him, the current too strong.

Soon he was selling opium to customers and propositioning tourists in the hotels. He even went so low as to actually help buy and sell young girls, some of them only nine and ten years old. It was a nasty business, and he was one of the most important of the young "businessmen."

Then the bottom dropped out of his world: He hit a string of bad luck. He was robbed, and while trying to climb back to the top, he was arrested. The word went out in the underworld that he was a police spy. He finally ended up living in a shanty by the city trashpile.

Sitting in his little shack, he thought about his family, especially his father, a simple Christian man from a small southern village near the Malaysian border. He remembered his dad's parting words: "I am waiting for you." He wondered whether his father would *still* be waiting for him after all that he had done to dishonor the family name. Would he be welcome in his home? Word of Sawat's lifestyle had long ago filtered back to the village.

Finally he devised a plan.

"Dear Father," he wrote, "I wanted to come home, but I don't know if you will receive me after all that I have done. I have sinned greatly, father. Please forgive me. On Saturday night

I will be on the train that goes through our village. If you are still waiting for me, will you tie a piece of cloth on the po tree in front of our house? (Signed) Sawat."

On that train ride he reflected on his life over the past few months and knew that his father had every right to deny him. As the train finally neared the village, he churned with anxiety. What would he do if there was no white cloth on the po tree?

Sitting opposite him was a kind stranger who noticed how nervous his fellow passenger had become. Finally Sawat could stand the pressure no longer. He blurted out his story in a torrent of words. As they entered the village, Sawat said, "Oh, sir, I cannot bear to look. Can you watch for me? What if my father will not receive me back?"

Sawat buried his face between his knees. "Do you see it, sir? It's the only house with a po tree."

"Young man, your father did not hang just *one* piece of cloth. Look! He has covered the whole tree with cloth!" Sawat could hardly believe his eyes. The branches were laden with tiny white squares. In the frontyard his old father jumped up and down, joyously waving a piece of white cloth, then ran in halting steps beside the train. When it stopped at the little station he threw his arms around his son, embracing him with tears of joy. "I've been waiting for you!'' he exclaimed.

Sawat's story poignantly parallels Jesus' parable of the Prodigal Son, found in Luke 15:11-24. Christ told of another son who threw his life and money away in a whirlwind of wrong choices and fearfully returned home in the hopes that his father would take him back. He too was met with the open arms, and was loved and accepted unconditionally. Three aspects of the Father heart of God emerge in both of these stories.

Freedom to Choose

The father loved his son enough to let him leave home.

Both fathers created the possibility for deep relationships with their sons through their willingness to allow the boys their freedom. Though inwardly the fathers grieved, they did not try to force a relationship. They simply made themselves available to serve as they had always done. This freedom was not granted because the sons agreed with their fathers, but because of love. They were wise enough to wait for the young men to want a relationship with them. Both fathers had spent years instructing their offspring in the ways they should go, but left the final choice to their sons.

These men's responses to their rebellious sons exemplify the heart of God. I believe He sovereignly chose to give man free will, and He took the risk of being rejected. God did not seek to establish an impersonal and involuntary obedience to a set of rules. He wanted heart-to-heart relationships with those whom He created. There is always a risk in giving people freedom of choice, but without that risk there can be no genuine love.

This kind of freedom can be violated if we do not give other people the same freedom God gives us. For us to try to force conformity, belief, or obedience through pressure, threats, or rules is to destroy the very heart of Christianity. When we move away from freedom, we enter into religious legalism, denying the grace of God.

Patiently Waiting

The father loved his son so deeply that he watched every day for him to return home.

A certain man came night after night to a large auditorium to hear a famous evangelist preach the gospel. Each evening he came, yet he was unmoved in his firm conviction that there was no reason to respond publicly to the appeals to make a commitment to Jesus Christ. "I can pray right here where I'm sitting," he reasoned. Yet he kept returning to hear more, always sitting in the same place.

Night after night a polite young man approached the well-to-do visitor and asked him if he would like to go forward to make a public commitment to follow Jesus Christ. Repeatedly the man told the young usher, "I can pray right here where I'm sitting. I don't need to go forward to pray or become a Christian!" To this the usher always responded courteously, "I'm sorry sir, but you are wrong. You cannot pray here. You must go forward if you want to make a commitment to accept Jesus Christ as your Lord and Savior." This conversation was repeated almost verbatim every night, but the businessman was determined not to respond with a show of "public emotion," as he called it.

Then came the last night of the meetings. The distinguished-looking man took the same seat he had occupied each evening. The evangelist preached and for the final time invited people in the audience to respond by coming to the front of the auditorium to indicate their desire to dedicate their lives to Jesus Christ. Once more the usher invited the man to walk up the aisle. "If you want to go to the front to give your life to Christ, I'll even go with you, sir," he volunteered.

This time the man looked up with tears in his eyes. He had been deeply touched by the preaching. He replied, "Oh, would you please go with me? I need to give my life to Christ. I'm ready to go forward and pray." The usher responded,

"Sir, you don't need to go forward to accept the Lord. You can pray right here where you are sitting!"

When this distinguished man was ready to humble himself, then the Lord could reach him where he was. The lost sons in the two stories finally came to the same point. When they finally acknowledged their guilt, then the change took place in their lives. The fathers longed for their sons to reach this attitude of sorrow for their sins, but knew it must be the young men's decision. Every day they watched for their sons and longed for their return. How great was their patience and compassion.

The sons could not blame their fathers for their problems. They ended up in poverty because of their own foolishness. When they realized their error, they repented and decided to return to their homes. In these stories, grace and repentance meet each other. Because the sons knew their fathers' love, they chose to admit their wrong and go home. Knowledge of that love finally brought them to repentance.

Our heavenly Father longs for us to return "home," whatever our problems, whatever our needs. Isaiah 30:18 says, "The Lord waits to be gracious to you." Romans 2:4 asks, "Do you not know that God's kindness is meant to lead you to repentance?"

He is the waiting Father.

Unconditional Acceptance

The father loved his son so much that when he did return home he did not condemn his son for his wrong actions, but he forgave him and celebrated his return with a great feast.

In the parable of the Prodigal Son, the father did more than wait. He ran! When he saw his dirty, weary son shuffling down the road, hesitant and uncertain, he hurried to him and embraced him. There was no reserve in his heart toward this one who had sinned. His joy revealed his complete forgiveness and acceptance.

God does not condone our rebellion or selfishness. It grieves Him deeply to see us hurting ourselves and others. Yet He constantly waits for us to respond to His love and receive His forgiveness. And when we do, He welcomes us freely and completely.

Knowing the Heart of God

As we think of God as the waiting Father, we must be careful not to think that His loving, forgiving attitude makes Him weak, or a "pushover." He is powerful and mighty above all others. There is great strength in His love. His ruthless hatred of evil tolerates no double-mindedness, but His compassion is endless toward those who see their need of Him. He sees our hearts. He knows our innermost thoughts.

He offers great security to all those who sincerely want to be in His family.

The Bible describes the character of our waiting Father in many ways. Consider some of the qualities which the Scriptures teach us about God.

1. *CREATOR:* One who creates us in His image with freedom to choose to freely respond to His love.

    "In him we live and move and have our being...for we are indeed his offspring" (Acts 17:28).

    "O Lord, thou art our Father; we are the clay and thou art our potter; we are all the work of thy hand" (Isaiah 64:8).

2. *PROVIDER:* One who loves to provide for our physical, emotional, mental, and spiritual needs.

    "If you then, who are evil, know how to give good gifts to your children, how much more will your Father who is in heaven give good gifts to those who ask him!" (Matthew 7:11).

3. *FRIEND AND COUNSELOR:* One who longs to have intimate friendship with us and to give us wise counsel and instruction.

    "Thou art the friend of my youth" (Jeremiah 3:4).

    "And his name will be called Wonderful, Counselor, Mighty God, Everlasting Father, Prince of Peace" (Isaiah 9:6).

"Thou doth guide me with thy counsel" (Psalm 73:24).

4. *CORRECTOR:* One who lovingly corrects and disciplines.

"My son, do not regard lightly the discipline of the Lord.... For the Lord disciplines him whom he loves, and chastises every son whom he receives.... If you are left without discipline...then you are illegitimate children and not sons.... For the moment all discipline seems painful rather than pleasant; later it yields the peaceful fruit of righteousness to those who have been trained by it" (Hebrews 12:5,6,8,11).

5. *REDEEMER:* One who forgives his children's faults and brings good out of their failures and weaknesses; One who saves.

"The Lord is merciful and gracious, slow to anger and abounding in steadfast love.... As far as the east is from the west, so far does he remove our transgressions from us. As a father pities his children, so the Lord pities those who fear him" (Psalm 103:8, 12,13).

6. *COMFORTER:* One who cares for us

and comforts us in times of need.

"Blessed be the God and Father of our Lord Jesus Christ, the Father of mercies and God of all comfort, who comforts us in all our afflictions" (2 Corinthians 1:3,4).

7. *DEFENDER AND DELIVERER:* One who loves to protect, defend, and deliver His children.

"He who dwells in the shelter of the Most High, who abides in the shadow of the Almighty, will say to the Lord, 'My refuge and my fortress; my God, in whom I trust.' For he will deliver you..." (Psalm 91:1-3).

8. *FATHER:* One who wants to free us from all false gods so that He can be a father to us.

"I will be a father to you, and you shall be my sons and daughters, says the Lord Almighty" (2 Corinthians 6:18).

9. *FATHER OF THE FATHERLESS:* One who cares for the homeless and the widow.

"Father of the fatherless and protector of widows is God in his holy habitation. God gives the desolate a home to dwell in" (Psalm 68:5,6).

10. *FATHER OF LOVE:* One who reveals Himself to us and reconciles us to Himself through Jesus Christ.

"The Father himself loves you, because you have loved me and have believed that I came from the Father" (John 16:27).

Despite all that the Bible teaches about God as loving and just, there was a time in my life when I respected Him but I did not love Him. I even feared Him because of His awesome power, but I did not love Him for His goodness.

It was when I looked beyond my ideas about God, beyond my desire to argue and discuss, and asked God to reveal to me how He saw my selfishness that I began to experience a deeper relationship with God.

God is a waiting, loving Father and so much more! As we spend time with Him, we will discover fresh insights into His character and new depths in our relationship with Him.

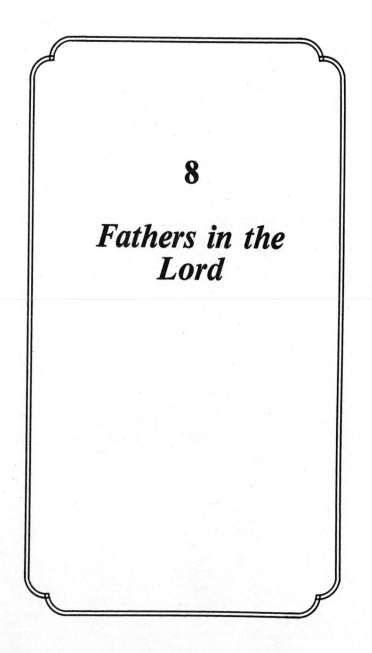

8

Fathers in the Lord

8

Fathers in the Lord

The world is filled with emotional and spiritual orphans.

Ali Agca was born in the remote mountain village of Yesiltepe in Turkey. He was just ten years old when his father died, and he smiled throughout the funeral. Ali hated his father passionately. The violent scenes of his father's brutality were seared permanently in his consciousness.

Shortly after his father's death, he made a "hate list" of people and things that had become the focus of his hostility. Only out of respect for his mother did Ali leave his father's name off the list.

Ali Agca grew up experiencing fits of depression accompanied by long periods of silence, withdrawal, and symptoms of anorexia nervosa. He suffered from guilt because of his hostility toward his father, and he ended up believing that hatred was the only channel through which he could purge himself of these feelings. He was an orphan left without the knowledge of love.

As a teenager he followed a path of tragedy and crime, including drug running and violence. He was involved in a school for terrorists in Lebanon, where people learned the latest "techniques of liberation."

On May 13, 1981, Mehmet Ali Agca's trail of terror ended abruptly, but not before broadcasters worldwide stumbled over the pronunciation of this unknown Turkish boy's name. He was identified as the man who, only hours before, had shot Pope John Paul II.

Now Ali Agca sits in a bare, white-walled cell in Rome's Rebibbia prison. It was to this cell that John Paul made his dramatic pilgrimage of forgiveness in late December, 1983. Although on one level it was an intensely intimate transaction between the two men, it was also a dramatic example of Christian charity. John Paul sat for 21 minutes, holding the hand that had held the gun. Whether one is Protestant or Catholic, it is impossible to deny the significance of John Paul's actions. What he did was profoundly *Christian*. He sought out his enemy and forgave him.

In so doing, he gave Ali Agca a new understanding of God and offered him a way out of the darkness and bitterness of his soul. During those 21 short minutes, John Paul, who said he spoke to Ali "...as a brother," showed him a way to the Father.

The Need for Fathers and Mothers in the Lord

So many people are orphaned, not just from their physical parents, but from any kind of healthy spiritual or emotional heritage. Earlier in this book I described the needs that many people have for healing. Pushed to the fringes of society by hurt and rejection, they feel alone in the world.

The church is also filled with spiritual orphans. Either they have accepted Jesus Christ but have not been nurtured in their faith, or because of some failure on their own or someone else's part they have not yet become a part of a spiritual family. They need a church *home*, a place where they belong.

These people desperately need pastoral care. They need to be taught God's Word, to be counseled with sound biblical principles, and to be encouraged and exhorted by someone mature in the faith. They need a spiritual father or mother who can help them grow in the Lord.

Others need to be "reparented"—that is, given the kind of example that only a wise, stable mother or father figure can provide. If proper parenting was missing during a person's developmental years, whether physically or spiritually or both, he or she needs someone to provide an example. This relationship should not revolve around a nagging or "hanging on," but should provide a role model that encourages growth.

Biblical Examples

Peter exhorted the elders to "tend the flock of God that is your charge" (1 Peter 5:2). Paul said to the Corinthian Christians that "though you have countless guides in Christ, you do not have many fathers.... Therefore I sent to you Timothy, my beloved and faithful child in the Lord, to remind you of my ways in Christ, as I teach them everywhere in every church" (1 Corinthians 4:15,17). Paul reminded the Thessalonians that "we were gentle among you, like a nurse taking care of her children.... For you know how, like a *father with his children*, we exhorted each one of you and encouraged you and charged you to lead a life worthy of God" (1 Thessalonians 2:7,11,12).

Being a father or mother in the Lord is not limited to those who are pastors or spiritual leaders. There is also a very crucial need for other spiritually mature, caring people to act as "fathers" and "mothers" to other believers. John speaks of those who are fathers in the Lord because "you know him who is from the beginning" (1 John 2:14). Young men like to fight Satan, but fathers know the *Father*. By their very presence they minister to those around them because of their maturity and depth in God. We need to turn loose these "moms and dads" in the church to be who they are. By being available, having time for people, and having an open home, their lives can be instruments of healing and love.

The Need for Balance

As in all areas, the emphasis on "spiritual fathering" can be carried to an extreme. The last thing people need today is abusive authority. The Bible speaks of equality, authority, and ministry, and it is important to distinguish the difference between these three concepts. Much confusion has resulted in the body of Christ because the proper distinctions have not been made.

Godly fathers want to serve others, and treat all men and women as their equals. Their actions proceed from an attitude of equality, not authority, because they are more concerned with serving than ruling. When one begins from an attitude of authority it is bound to result in an attitude of superiority or a kind of paternalism that can become dominating and suffocating.

The following chart helps point out the differences between the two approaches.

Dominating Fathers	Fathers in the Lord
1. Function as if *they* are the source of guidance for people's lives.	1. Believe that God is the source of guidance and desire to help other Christians learn to hear His voice.
2. Emphasize the *rights* of leaders.	2. Emphasize the *responsibilities* of leaders.
3. Set leaders apart and give them special privileges.	3. Emphasize the body of Christ serving one another, with the Lord as the focus.
4. Seek to control people's actions.	4. Encourage people to be dependent on God.
5. Emphasize the importance of the leaders ministering to others.	5. Emphasize the importance of equipping the saints for the work of the ministry.
6. Use rules and laws to control people and force them to conform to a mold.	6. Provide an atmosphere of trust and grace to encourage spiritual growth.
7. Confront sin on the level of outward actions and group conformity.	7. Confront sin on the level of heart attitude and brokenness before God.
8. Stress the uniqueness of "our" group, constantly emphasizing special revelation that God has given to their group and not others.	8. Stress the importance of unity with the whole body of Christ and the importance of keeping a humble attitude toward others.

9. Judge people's responses to God on how consistently they see things from the leader's point of view. Discourage diversity of thought and action.

9. Realize the importance of an individual's heart attitude toward God, not just his or her doctrinal conformity, as a basis of unity.

Biblical authority is never taken; it is offered. It does not reside in a position or a right. It is the outworking of who we are, not of an office we hold or a title that appears on our door. It comes from the anointing of God's Spirit and is the sum total of one's character, wisdom, spiritual gift, and servant attitude.

Fathers in the Lord understand these principles about authority. They know the character of the *Father*, so they are relaxed in their ministry to other people. This does not mean they are indecisive and unable to confront people when necessary. Rather, they have learned to take action as God directs, and not just because they are "the leader."

Receiving from Fathers in the Lord

It takes humility to receive from someone. When God brings a person into our lives to teach us, we must have the right attitude so we can benefit from all that God wants to do in us through that person.

God longs to comfort us and encourage us through others, but His love is blocked if we do not have a teachable attitude and a heart that is open to accept what He wants to give us. To think that we do not need to receive from others does not prove humility or maturity; it reveals pride. We do, however, have the final responsibility before God to discern if what others say to us is correct. We cannot agree with people if we do not have the conviction they are right. The Bible is our measuring stick as we evaluate the counsel of others.

There is a difference between a submissive spirit and absolute obedience. Absolute obedience is given only to God, submission is given to man. Submission involves an attitude of openness to receive from someone else. God is the only One worthy of total allegiance.

When several of David's brave soldiers overheard him say that he longed for a drink of water from the wells of Bethlehem, they decided to get it for him. The wells, however, were within the camp of the Philistines, David's enemies. So these men fought their way into the camp in a daring raid, risking their lives to get David some of that precious well water.

Imagine the look on their faces as they staggered back into camp, wounded and bleeding, bursting with pride at their accomplishment. To their great dismay, David took the water they offered and poured it on the gound! "Devotion such as this," he declared, "belongs only to the Lord."

David recognized the potential for his men to give him the devotion due only to God, and he wisely redirected their loyalties. Hurt as they must have been, years later those same mighty men told others of the lesson David had taught them about keeping God first in their lives. In the long run he earned their respect.

To be "fathered" or "mothered" in the Lord does not mean that we have to enter a formal, defined relationship with a mature Christian. Sometimes it just means watching their lives. Other times it means asking questions or seeking counsel.

Jesus fathered His disciples in four stages:
1. He did the work and they watched.
2. He did the work and they helped.
3. They did the work and He helped.
4. They did the work and He left!

Fathering Other People

Being a good father, whether in the church or the home, has more to do with the atmosphere we create than the words we speak. People will remember our attitudes and actions, *how* we say things, far longer than our actual conversations. Those attitudes, and our underlying philosophies of life and ministry, set a mood everywhere we go. We take it with us.

For example, some people freely express their love and concern for us. They convey it in many little but obvious ways, and it isn't long before we feel free to be open and honest with them. With others, however, we wouldn't tell them something personal even if they pledged secrecy and trustworthiness.

Obviously, it is important to get more specific than just saying we should create a nice atmosphere. Otherwise all we would need to do is keep the lights soft, burn some candles, play the right music, and presto—spiritual "atmosphere." Spiritual atmosphere involves the life principles demonstrated through our words and actions. It is not created by accident; it is the by-product of the entirety of our lives.

Some enemies of the great nineteenth-century evangelist Charles Finney tried to embarrass him on one occasion by asking him to speak at a large pastor's conference without prior warning. Finney graciously accepted their last-minute invitation and spoke powerfully for 1½ hours! Afterward a young student asked him how long it had taken him to prepare his sermon. "Young man," Finney replied, "I have been preparing that sermon for the last 20 years!"

Following are some of the ingredients that contribute to an atmosphere of love and trust.

>We create an atmosphere for spiritual growth through the love and trust we share with other people.
>We create an atmosphere of belonging

by including others in important decisions.

We create an atmosphere of responsibility by trusting others.

We create an atmosphere of compassion through our courtesy and kindness.

We create an atmosphere of godliness and spiritual reality by meditating regularly on God's Word and by practicing a personal worship of God.

We create an atmosphere of faith and vision by seeing needs and discerning God's response to the need.

We create an atmosphere of generosity by giving to other people.

We create an atmosphere of righteousness by acknowledging God's power for every situation.

We create an atmosphere of human value and worth by taking time to listen.

We create an atmosphere of self-esteem by affirming and encouraging others.

We create an atmosphere of comfort by caring when others are hurt.

We create an atmosphere of team unity by sincerely desiring to involve others in ministry, praying that their works will be greater than ours.

We create an atmosphere of joy and peace by expressing our thankfulness and gratefulness to God in every situation.

We create an atmosphere of security by

recognizing the good and the potential in others.

We create an atmosphere of obedience to God by valuing His standards more than man's.

We create an atmosphere of loyalty by never criticizing others.

We create an atmosphere of faith by telling of the greatness of God.

We create an atmosphere of honesty by admitting our weaknesses and asking for forgiveness for our wrongs.

If we as parents or spiritual leaders have hurt our children or those we lead, we should seriously pray about making restitution. They need to hear us say we are sorry and we need to hear them say we are forgiven. It is not enough to "let bygones be bygones." When we humble ourselves in this manner, it often opens the door to healing and reconciliation and leads to deeper relationships and understanding.

What greater inheritance can we offer to others? As we give the gifts of compassion and humility, our lives become demonstrations of the truth of God's Word. We create an atmosphere of grace, and build a highway of love between our hearts and the hearts of other people. Our willingness to be used as God's vessels can make His tender Father-heart a reality to our hurting world.

EPILOGUE

As I mentioned earlier, I have been called by God to serve Him and other people in the inner city of Amsterdam, Holland. Our family is part of a wonderful community of people who love God and who have found their fulfillment in life by serving Him in this city.

We have found that the principles and truths described in this book really work. And we are learning more every day. Serving God is a wonderful adventure, especially when you are a part of a missionary community, a family of brothers and sisters learning to make the Father's love a reality both to one another and to those who do not know Him.

We are also part of an international, inter-denominational organization dedicated to sharing the gospel in many different nations of the world. If you have been helped by this book and it has motivated you to want to help others, there are many opportunities for service. Your service to God and others should begin where you are, but if you are also interested in helping other people in a place like Amsterdam or one of the other great cities in our world for a summer, a year, or even longer, please write to us and ask for information about opportunities for service. We also run three-month training programs in counseling, biblical studies, basis discipleship, leadership training, and cross-cultural missions. We also offer a two-year degree through the School of Urban Missions, designed for those who desire in-depth training in reaching urban sociological and ethnic groups. If you would like more information on how to get involved in any of these programs, write to:

Urban Missions Project
Youth With a Mission
Prins Hendrikkade 50
1012 AC Amsterdam
The Netherlands

If you are in need of further counseling, please contact:

John Dawson
c/o YWAM
P.O. Box 296
Sunland, CA 91040-0296

APPENDIX

Guidelines for Selecting a
Psychologist or Counselor

Unfortunately, poorly skilled people often prey on sincere Christians by calling themselves counselors. A well-trained counselor or psychologist can be extremely helpful, but it is important to be sure that he or she is well-qualified and is supportive of the Christian faith. Following are three basic guidelines to follow when choosing a counselor or psychologist.

1. The best way to select a counselor or psychologist is to rely on a referral from a respected church leader, family doctor, or friend who has had previous contact with the professional and knows him or her personally.

2. Competent professionals are not threatened if a prospective patient calls and tactfully asks about their qualifications, their theoretical orientation, their experience with the particular problem at hand, and the type of license they hold.

3. Fees should be discussed in advance of any commitment to treatment.

We should not expect counselors or psychologists to fulfill the role of spiritual leaders, but these professionals can be effective instruments in the healing process in their area of expertise.

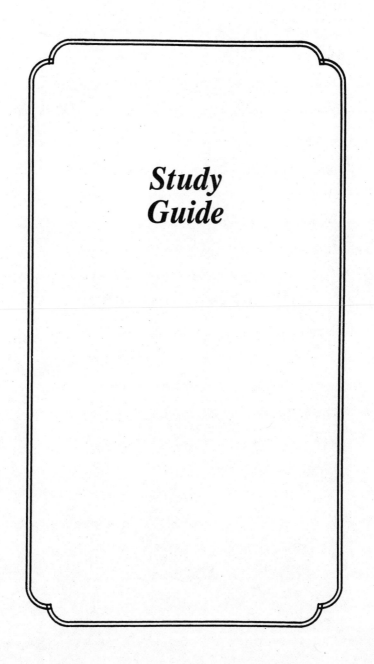

*Study
Guide*

Chapter 1:
THE HURTING HEART OF MAN

Read John 1 & 2

1. Describe your personal concept of Father God. What is He like to you? Be as honest and specific as you can.

2. Do you have a personal/intimate relationship with Him?

3. What are your *feelings* toward your earthly father?

4. Do you have a personal/intimate relationship with him?

5. Do you trust your earthly father? If no, can you reason why and identify those areas of mistrust? List them.

6. Do you trust Father God? If no, can you reason why and identify those areas of mistrust? List them.

7. List as many Scripture references as you can in which Jesus describes the heart of the Father.

8. Read John 14:8-11. What do you sense the Lord saying to you?

9. Unhealed emotional wounds = wounded/broken spirit = bitterness/hate. Have you ever *felt* rejected by or alienated from family, friends, co-workers or the church? If yes, describe the incident(s).

10. Do you think you are walking in a degree of hurt from that rejection/alienation at this time? If yes, describe how it affects you today.

11. The only healing for this condition is

—————————————————————————.

Are you willing to be led by the Father's love into a walk of forgiveness, thereby healing your emotional wounds?

Chapter 2:
A PERFECT FATHER

Read John 3 & 4

1. Describe your family environment during your childhood. Was there peace, joy, stability, security, strife, depression, etc.?

2. Did you *feel* loved and accepted? Wanted? Valuable? Special?

3. Are you aware Father God created families so He would be glorified by the fruit produced in this loving, secure environment? Was He glorified in your family? Explain.

4. List the male authority figures in your life, and how you felt toward them.

5. Did/do you trust these men?

6. Did/do you feel you were important to these men?

7. Did/do you receive much physical affection from these men?

8. List some of the most painful moments of your life. Beside those moments, write the name of a male authority figure who showed love and compassion when you hurt.

9. Where was God during the painful times of your life?

10. List the people (male or female) who have loved you unconditionally.

11. Are you able to *receive* unconditional love from the creator of love—Father God?

12. Do you feel you have been hurt in one of the seven areas of parental love? If you aren't sure, ask someone close to you. Be as specific as you can in identifying this area of hurt.

13. Are you willing to forgive anyone who has hurt you? Be honest.

Chapter 3:
WHEN YOUR HEART IS WOUNDED

Read John 5 & 6

1. How can our selfishness separate us from Father God?

As you review the pages dealing with the "Saul Syndrome," seriously reflect on your own life, your personality, your feelings. Consider if there is any correlation between you and Saul. It is often wise to seek the insight of your spouse or close friend when doing this, as they often see things in our lives we cannot . . . especially in dealing with question 12.

2. Do you believe God the Father sent Jesus Christ into the world to introduce a ministry of reconciliation, to end forever the separation of man (that includes you) from Father God? (2 Cor. 5:16-21).

3. Do you believe that through Jesus Christ, healing can replace woundedness, and that you can walk in wholeness rather than brokenheartedness? How can this happen?

4. List areas in your life where you feel insecure.

5. Do you have a servant heart? How is this expressed?

6. Are you willing to humble yourself and take the lower road? When?

7. Do you feel either frequent or uncontrolled anger? When?

8. Do you have bouts of melancholy and/or depression? What triggers them?

9. Are you (inwardly) impressed with your "authority"?

10. Does your sense of value and worth depend on praise from others? What happens if you don't receive that praise?

11. Do you have a greater fear of (desire to please) God than man? In what areas of your life is this true?

12. Study the characteristics of Saul's personality: Inferiority; Stubbornness or Independence; Pride; Fear of man; Disobedience. Do you recognize any of them in your life?

13. Describe the Saul Syndrome traits you see in yourself. This is also an excellent time to ask someone close to you what they see.

   Withdrawal or isolation
   Possessiveness
   Us-versus-them mentality
   Manipulation
   Unteachableness
   Critical and judgmental attitudes
   Impatience
   Distrust
   Disloyalty
   Ingratitude
   Unhealthy idealism

14. What is the difference between "power" and "authority"?

15. What does having the "fear of the Lord" mean to you?

16. What is the author's definition of humility?

17. What are the benefits of walking in a greater fear of God than of man?

Chapter 4:
HEALING FROM A LOVING FATHER

Read John 7-8-9

It is important that you find a private place and adequate time for this lesson.

Before you begin this section, review the previous three lessons. Any questions you have not fully answered should be done at this time. As you re-read them, it is likely the Lord will give you even greater insight.

Now it is important to ask yourself, "Am I ready to assume responsibility for actions/reactions in the area(s) the Father reveals to me, and to ask His forgiveness for selfishness and rebellion against Him?"

This is not meant to make light of the pain and hurt you may have encountered in your life. Rather it is meant to show that how we respond, often to protect ourselves, is frequently not Christ-centered. In these cases, we need to recognize our sin and seek our Father's forgiveness.

It is best to be as specific as you can when recalling these incidents and confessing your wrong responses in detail to your loving Father God.

Guidelines for Emotional Healing

- Acknowledge your need of healing. Admit you need help.
  - Be honest with the Father. He will then be able to comfort and guide you.
  - Confess your sins. These sins should be confessed *only* on the level they were committed.

    Secret sin—A sin of the heart or mind that was never acted on or spoken out to others. Needs to be confessed only to the Father.

    Private sin—Ask forgiveness of the one you have sinned against.

    Public sin—Ask the group's forgiveness.
  - Confess your negative emotions—feelings of anger, fear, bitterness, disappointment, resentment, etc. Even *no* emotion being shown can be as harmful as a negative emotion. Always talk to Jesus first, then to others if need be.

— Forgive those who have hurt you. Most often this is a process, not a one-time act.
— Receive forgiveness. Ask and receive the Father's forgiveness for your wrong actions and/or attitudes toward others.
— Receive the Father's love. Spend time in His presence.
— Think God's thoughts—not negative, defensive, selfish thoughts. Break old patterns of how you think about yourself. When you begin to think a negative thought, stop and say God's truth about that thought and find a Scripture to back it up.
— Endure. Giving up makes us vulnerable to negative feelings. Read and memorize Philippians 1:6.

It might be a good idea for you to make a list of the specific things you are asking the Father to forgive. You will probably then see a pattern in your life that, when recognized and repented of, can be altered by your Father. It is not important for you to keep this list, as it could cause embarrassment if read by someone else, but it could be helpful to you initially.

REMEMBER—Emotional healing is almost always a process. It takes time.

It is of paramount importance that you do not turn to people and focus on them as the source of healing. Your Heavenly Father is the only one capable of totally healing you. Disappointment comes from wanting people to heal you, and them not being able to do what God alone can do.

Chapter 5:
THE HEART OF
DISAPPOINTMENT

Read John 10-11-12

1. On a scale of 1 to 10, how often do you experience the feeling of disappointment? (1 = never – 10 = always)

2. How do you handle disappointment? Does it make you mad, afraid, embarrassed, hurt, discouraged, unbelieving, etc.? List *all* the feelings you experience when disappointed.

3. Disappointments can result in tremendous personal growth and a deeper spiritual understanding. Are you at a place where you can ask the Father why He has caused or allowed a disappointing situation, and what He wants you to learn in the midst of it?

4. Do you see yourself as having unrealistic expectations for other people—therefore causing your own disappointment? List those people

who disappoint you most, and describe how they do so.

5. As we learn to deal with one another's

_____,
we will overcome the unrealistic expectations that caused disappointment in the past.

6. What kind of attitude are we to have in responding to each and every circumstance? Explain why, and what that attitude can cause.

7. We, like David, need to learn to

_____

ourselves in order to be receptive to God's purpose(s) for us in the midst of disappointment. How can you best do that?

8. What is the greatest barrier to learning through difficulty and disappointment? Explain why.

9. Pages 86 and 87 list 15 symptoms of pride. Discuss these symptoms with the Father and with your spouse or close friend to see if any of them are evident in your life. List those that pertain to you. Pray that you will have an open heart during this time, to see areas you need to deal with.

10. Explain how setting expectations on other people, causing us to focus on them or ourselves rather than on the Lord, can produce broken relationships.

11. Read and reread the questions on page 91. Become so familiar with them that the next time you are disappointed, you will ask them to yourself and be able to grow and learn from the disappointment rather than to suffer in self-pity (PRIDE).

Chapter 6:
THE BROKEN HEART OF GOD

Read John 13-14-15

1. Explain how God intended man to live with Him *eternally* at the very beginning of creation.

2. Do you see how sin and selfishness make man today so completely different than how God created him to be? Explain.

3. Referring to question #2, who is the most broken over what has happened, man or God? Explain.

4. What is Godly sorrow based on, and what does it produce?

5. What does repentance involve?

6. Do feelings and selfish motives move us into Godly sorrow? Why or why not?

7. God created us to have fellowship with Him, and through that love relationship obedience would be a natural result. Therefore, our obedience to our Father God should come as a

   _____.

8. If the non-believers in your family or among your friends had a true concept of God, do you think they would become believers?

9. Do you see how wrong God-concepts have caused many to reject Him and His love?

10. What can you do to reveal truth to non-believers in your family and among your friends?

11. List some of the hypocrisy and injustice you see in the church today.

12. Can you see hypocrisy in your life? Ask your spouse or someone close to you what they "see." Are you willing to begin dealing with hypocrisy in the church by first dealing with it in your own life?

13. Even though other people's actions against you may have been wrong and caused you pain and hurt, are you willing to be responsible for and deal with your own sinful attitudes and reactions? Tell how this approach could change your life.

Chapter 7: THE WAITING FATHER

Read John 16-17-18

1. Read Luke 15:11-24. Insert your name in this story of the parable of the Prodigal Son. Can you identify with any of the characters in this parable? Which one(s)?

2. Explain in your own words how there can be no sincere, honest love without the freedom of choice.

3. "... God's kindness leads you toward repentance." (Romans 2:4). Without an awareness of this truth, do you see how it would be very difficult to acknowledge your guilt and humble yourself in an act of repentance? Explain how this has proven true in your life.

4. Explain the importance of allowing people around you, even those you deeply love, the freedom to go their own way, that they might come to their point of need.

5. Are you willing to wait, with a loving heart attitude, for those who have hurt and disappointed you, and then to *welcome* them home? Ask God to give you the name of one such person you can begin praying for now.

6. Of the 10 qualities of God listed on pages 119-122, make a list of the ones you know to be true and another for those you are not certain of yet. Then ask the Father to cause those uncertainties to become truth to you.

Chapter 8:
FATHERS IN THE LORD

Read John 19-20-21

1. Describe the difference between dominating fathers and "Fathers in the Lord."

2. Godly fathers should always be more concerned with _____ than with _____.

3. Are you willing to be a "Father in the Lord" to whomever the Lord would send you?

4. Our Father God has and will continue to put people in our lives to father us. Are you willing to receive what the Lord would have for you from a "Father in the Lord"?

5. Explain the importance of total allegiance to God and not to man.

6. The _____ should always be the measuring stick we use to evaluate the counsel of others.

7. What is "spiritual atmosphere," and what does it involve?

RECOMMENDED READING

The Forgotten Father. Thomas A. Smail, Hodder and Stoughton, London.

Transformation of the Inner Man. John Sanford, Bridge Publishing, Inc.

How to Really Love Your Child. Ross Campbell, Victor Books.

The Effective Father. Gordon MacDonald, Tyndale.

Healing for Damaged Emotions. David Seamands, Victor Books.

Putting Away Childish Things. David Seamands, Victor Books.

Dropping Your Guard. Charles Swindoll, Word.

Effective Biblical Counseling. Lawrence Crabb, Jr., Zondervan.

Father Care. Charles Paul Conn, Word.

Other Good
Harvest House Reading

GOD'S BEST FOR MY LIFE
by *Lloyd John Ogilvie*

Not since Oswald Chambers' *My Utmost for His Highest* has there been such an inspirational yet easy-to-read devotional. Dr. Ogilvie provides guidelines for maximizing your prayer and meditation time.

IN TOUCH WITH GOD
How God Speaks to a Prayerful Heart
by *Marie Shropshire*

Knowing how to have life-giving fellowship with God in the midst of life's challenges is the key to fulfillment in the Christian walk. From this personal journal we learn that there is no difficulty or wound that is out of reach of His healing touch.

QUIET MOMENTS FOR WOMEN
by *June Masters Bacher*

Though written for women, this devotional will benefit the entire family. Mrs. Bacher's down-to-earth, often humorous experiences have a daily message of God's love for you!

SECRET INVASION
by *Hans Kristian and Dave Hunt*

Secret Invasion traces one man's incredible journey from pastor to "spy, thief, and robber"—the labels placed on Hans Kristian by interrogators as he tirelessly smuggled Bibles into Russia. This suspense-filled true story will leave you astounded at the power of God to guide this brave young pastor and to provide for persecuted Christians in Russia and Eastern Europe.

Dear Reader:

We would appreciate hearing from you regarding this Harvest House nonfiction book. It will enable us to continue to give you the best in Christian publishing.

1. What most influenced you to purchase *The Father Heart of God*?
   ☐ Author   ☐ Recommendations
   ☐ Subject matter   ☐ Cover/Title
   ☐ Backcover copy   ☐ _____

2. Where did you purchase this book?
   ☐ Christian bookstore   ☐ Grocery store
   ☐ General bookstore   ☐ Other
   ☐ Department store

3. Your overall rating of this book:
   ☐ Excellent ☐ Very good ☐ Good ☐ Fair ☐ Poor

4. How likely would you be to purchase other books by this author?
   ☐ Very likely   ☐ Not very likely
   ☐ Somewhat likely   ☐ Not at all

5. What types of books most interest you?
   (check all that apply)
   ☐ Women's Books   ☐ Fiction
   ☐ Marriage Books   ☐ Biographies
   ☐ Current Issues   ☐ Children's Books
   ☐ Self Help/Psychology   ☐ Youth Books
   ☐ Bible Studies   ☐ Other _____

6. Please check the box next to your age group.
   ☐ Under 18   ☐ 25-34   ☐ 45-54
   ☐ 18-24   ☐ 35-44   ☐ 55 and over

Mail to: Editorial Director
Harvest House Publishers
1075 Arrowsmith
Eugene, OR 97402

Name _____

Address _____

City _____ State _____ Zip _____

Thank you for helping us to help you in future publications!